TEACHING WITH THE CONNECTION FACTOR

Joy Straner

and

Beth Bloodworth Threlkeld

SMYTHE PRESS

TEACHING WITH THE CONNECTION FACTOR

ISBN-13: 978-0-9821778-1-5
ISBN-10: 0-9821778-1-X

Library of Congress Control Number: 2009930297

Published by Smythe Press
a division of TexVest Partners LLC
www.smythepress.com

PRINTED IN THE UNITED STATES OF AMERICA

Dedication

For our family members who helped mold our past and present:

Joe, Becky, Hope and Michael from Joy

Jim, Richard, Kitty, Peggy F., Dick, Kap, Amy, Katie, Bobby,
Peggy V. and David from Beth

For the young people in our lives who will help mold the future:

Chase, Hunter and Trey from Joy

Meg, Nick, Libby, Katharine, Allie, Leslie and
Kathleen from Beth

Introduction

Education is ever changing, and with this change comes an overwhelming need to adjust the way we DO education. Often teachers get lost in the quicksand of required paperwork and the murky waters of textbooks, manuals, and standards instead of concentrating on the young people and what they need. Our concern about the difficulty of reaching every child and meeting their needs led us to collect important data that we will share with you.

We surveyed 100 teachers who varied in professional experience, grade levels, and school systems. We asked two questions:

In your instruction and facilitating of learning, do you find that it is important to connect with your students in order to help them perform more successfully?

In your efforts to connect with your students, how do you rate the success of your efforts to connect with every student every time you present a lesson?

Question One showed that 92% of the teachers surveyed felt that connecting with their students was Very Important; 8% said Important. Question Two resulted in 52% rating their efforts as Not Successful in connecting to every student every time; 44% said they experienced Fair Success.

This outcome told us that teachers value the importance of connecting to students, but they find it challenging to accomplish that connection with every student every time in order to help them perform successfully. Thus, the rationale for this book was formed.

Simply put, we want to help teachers make the most of The Connection Factor, a principle that involves connecting with each student while teaching.

Teaching with the Connection Factor:
In Search of Serendipity

Chapter 1
Principle of Serendipity

"Accidental gifts do not come to the idle, but to those who are actively pursuing goals. The word, serendip, is the ancient Arabian name for Sri Lanka. A fairy tale is told of King Fafer of Serendip, who sent his three prince sons out to broaden their education. The three princes were always searching for one thing but finding something else – a serendipity – that was better than what they had originally hoped to find" (Godwin, 2000).

It is our suggestion that the concept of serendipity is an effective way to approach teaching: a teacher lays out well thought-out plans with possible options as places to go with the topic. Then the drama unfolds as students become excited about learning more about the subject matter. A teacher can actually be pleasantly surprised when students buy in to their learning and become responsible decision makers regarding their unit of study.

Think about the teacher in your youth who stands out in your memory as being the most extraordinary teacher you had. Hopefully, there's at least one who comes to mind! Now reflect on one specific trait that makes this teacher stand out. Could it be the way this teacher made you feel? – That he or she really listened to you? – Did this teacher encourage you to think big about your capabilities? – Make you feel smart, creative or just plain worthy of his/her time, giving you a sense of self value? Surely we would not recall a past teacher as being outstanding or effective if he/she was unapproachable or if he/she made us feel badly about ourselves. We will assume that in some way, most extraordinary teachers reveal a particular characteristic which we will call The Connection Factor. This factor refers to a teacher who makes a point to connect with students. Connecting or being tuned in to perceive student interest is HOW serendipity can occur. When serendipity takes place, it is our belief that students retain more knowledge and skills because they have taken ownership for their learning which increases their comprehension and purpose and drives their learning.

Whether you did or did not remember a teacher who exhibited this Connection Factor, please know that you can have it. You can make a deliberate choice to obtain this trait. Our aim is to convince you that, if you do not possess this characteristic, you have it in your power to develop it.

In this book, we will show how Serendipity Teaching through The Connection Factor works. This approach is effective for all ages, all subjects, all ability levels, and various stages of English. Additionally, students with behavior and learning disorders are often more successful when they sense their teachers care enough to tune in to meet their needs. We will share our personal ideas and experiences as well as those whom we have researched. Getting the big idea of serendipity is going to make a difference in your teaching. This practice will make learning more spontaneous and successful for your students – improving students' retention of knowledge and skills.

By using Serendipity Teaching we are not suggesting that learning should be unstructured, unplanned, or strictly by chance. Rather, we are saying that there still needs to be well thought out lessons correlated with standards that will guide your instruction towards your wanted outcome. With this in place, you have the framework established to veer into those wonderful, teachable moments that come up in your classroom by connecting with your students. Serendipity is not something that will appear in every lesson, but setting the stage for this possibility is something to be cognizant of as you plan your lesson or unit.

If you grasp the concept of Serendipity Teaching, our hope is that you will find your planning and execution of lessons will become an extension of your classroom community's interests and excitement about a given topic. Let's go forward on our adventure together to learn more about Serendipity Teaching. We will show you how to successfully utilize this concept. It will be worth your while!

As the Serendip princes set out to find their gifts, certain factors needed to be in place for a successful journey. Obviously if the journey was well-planned, there was a better chance for good results. Today's classroom experience is no different. Within the parameters of planning effective teaching, certain attributes we believe should be in place. For the sake of serendipity (accidental gifts found while actively pursuing goals), setting the stage for teaching is vital to the results.

Thus, we now will discuss how to turn mediocre teaching into extraordinary teaching. It is imperative to have certain jewels in place to enable these accidental gifts to be found on your journey. You will see that these jewels are not necessarily new ideas, but they are considered to be important based on the experiences of the authors.

Five jewels for effective classroom instruction

- Creating a nurturing, learning, community environment
- Utilizing flexibility in teaching and learning
- Perceiving students' enthusiasm for learning
- Teaching to higher thinking
- Using cooperative learning and interactive processing

Below we have included brief discussions of each of our "five jewels" because we feel upholding them lays the groundwork for successful teaching. Without these factors in place, Serendipity Teaching is unlikely to occur. After this foundation has been set, we can go forward with HOW Serendipity Teaching and Learning can take place. As we focus on each jewel, let us think about the importance of each in the educational setting.

First, let's look at Creating a Nurturing Learning Environment. "School is a concept wherein students are welcome to learn and enhance the quality of their lives without fear of intimidation or harm, guided by hospitable and caring people in a clean and orderly environment" (Wong, Harry K. and Rosemary T., 2001). To provide a safe environment, the first key component is having a good classroom management plan in place. It is difficult to create a successful learning environment if there are unnecessary distractions from students within the classroom.

Staying positive and patient can be challenging, but is vital. Disciplining fairly is also important and not necessarily easy. When establishing a classroom management plan, you need to consider the consequences you are going to instill to go along with the possible misbehaviors in your classroom so that each day your classroom runs as smoothly and consistently as possible.

"Discipline is tricky because you have to individualize every situation based on reasons for misbehaviors and past offenses while still weighing the severity of the misbehavior and being fair. Keep your expectations as clear as possible. Listen closely and weigh your decisions carefully as you monitor your reinforcement and reward system cautiously. However, you will soon discover that exceptions occur and rules have to be broken. When this happens, you have to discuss the situations with your students, so they understand your reasoning. And, at times, you may have to say that you have made a decision because you are the teacher with no more explanation. In some situations, you must maintain confidentiality and silence. Whew! It isn't easy.

And watch out! Our experience tells us that most teachers are more likely to notice and punish misbehaviors than to notice and reward desired behaviors. Perhaps it is human nature to be disturbed by what is wrong rather than appreciating what is right. Be aware of your attitudes and approaches. You may discover that you are picking on some students and letting other students slide by. Duane, age 9, grade 3 says not to make everyone lose recess when a few people misbehave..." (Kottler and Gallavan, 2007).

Many education professionals have suggested that it is not a bad idea to have students help with establishing the classroom rules for the year. We believe this gives students ownership in the classroom management plan and provides a higher level of accountability among students towards making the plan successful. If you have not tried this before, take a risk – you just might be surprised with the ideas they have and the choices your students will make!

Hopefully, we have made it evident that to be effective in the classroom, you must have a management plan in place and make it part of your classroom instruction from day one. While guidelines are important to a classroom management plan, please understand that each plan is a work in progress. "It (the plan) needs to be taught, not assumed," states Dr. Gene Pease (2008). These plans may need to be adjusted and continually taught throughout the year, as well as changed at the beginning of each year. It all depends on the make-up of your class. In regards to using a reward system in your classroom, it should be noted that a "reward" can be something as simple as a positive comment to a child, as opposed to creating an elaborate reward system of tangible items. YOU are the teacher; you need to figure out what is best for your students!

Remember the Wongs' advice that "school...is guided by hospitable and caring people..." If a teacher's classroom management plan is not carried out with a nurturing component, the response may be less effective. Every student needs to know that someone cares about them and their success. In some cases that person may only be a child's teacher.

While speaking of a nurturing environment, we want to point out that our diverse population needs to be considered. Students come from varied backgrounds including different economics, cultures, family dynamics, races, languages, etc. All students need to feel comfortable and safe in their surroundings to promote success. The component of addressing a culturally diverse classroom will be discussed in more detail in Chapter Four.

Previously, we have discussed the first jewel of effective classroom instruction which told about the importance of behavior management and how it affects the classroom experience; this will be the only discussion on discipline within the book. The next four jewels will be intertwined within the remaining chapters of our book. Now, we will simply define each jewel and discuss it briefly.

The second jewel emphasizes the importance of flexibility. It is very important that teachers are able to bend accordingly with each lesson, activity, or incident. In the real world of education, things do not always turn out the way we plan or envision them. When lessons begin taking a turn in a different direction, the teacher does not need to view this as a negative because it may actually create a better situation than planned. Another way to view flexibility is when your planned project presentations are interrupted by an afternoon fire drill; you just have to make do. So, what if those presentations don't get finished on Friday? You can finish them on Monday. There is something to be said about the expression "going with the flow". Sometimes that is just what you have to do! When you are okay with interruptions, your children will be also. Flexibility is the key to happy and successful teaching and learning.

The third jewel deals with perceiving students' enthusiasm. The best scenario for this is when you, an extraordinary teacher, make a conscientious effort to remain "in tune" with your students' strengths and weaknesses, likes and dislikes, and excitement about the content. This perception will guide you in making decisions about activities and the direction your lesson or unit will take. When a teacher is aware of students' interests or lack of such and adjusts accordingly, he/she is making an effort to be an effective teacher in the classroom by respecting students as real people. This attribute places the teacher above the ordinary!

In preparing plans for your classroom lessons, you need to note that all ability and language levels need to be challenged with each activity. It is vital that you teach your students to think creatively and critically. For some time it has been widely known that companies prefer employees who are good problem solvers and can think through each job-related concern independently and critically. This has become a priority in the field of education. Therefore, the fourth jewel for effective classroom instruction is teaching students to think at higher levels.

Another significant aspect to students' success in the future is working and learning cooperatively with others along with interactive processing. This skill is our fifth jewel as we strive to teach our students the necessity of working together. Additionally, cooperative learning is significant in that it increases our knowledge base by integrating thoughts and ideas with those of classmates. Therefore, the old adage that two minds are better than one actually becomes a reality. Also, imperative to learning is presenting opportunities to actively interact within the content of the lesson. This interaction can be with other students, with the teacher, with objects within the lesson such as manipulatives, and can sometimes be an individual component if students are involved in research or other project-related activities. Within this particular jewel teachers have opportunities to create activities for cooperative efforts in learning as well as giving students a challenge of independent growth as they expand their learning and knowledge.

So, you may ask, how do these five jewels relate to the concept of serendipity? Without the five jewels, in our opinion, effective teaching does not occur. Without effective teaching, serendipity will not take place. For instance, you cannot get anywhere in the classroom without first establishing a learning environment that exudes a caring community atmosphere where students will feel free to explore and expand their knowledge base. Flexibility and perceiving students' enthusiasm allows you to actually put serendipity in place as you open your eyes and ears to the students' aptitude in regards to your lesson. This awareness enables you, the teacher, to know whether you have come to a green light (saying "GO!"), red light ("STOP, this is not working!"), or a yellow light (indicating, "CAUTION: better rethink my direction"). Finally, gearing your instruction to incorporate higher level thinking skills, along with creating opportunities for students to learn cooperatively and interactively, will permit them to go places far beyond even your imagination.

THAT'S SERENDIPITY

The Connection Factor:
Applying the Jewels to Foster Serendipitous Moments

Chapter 2
Lesson Launchers

Have you ever been in a class setting where the teacher just goes on and on, reading from a book or lecturing in that monotone voice and you want to run out of the room screaming because you can't take it anymore? It's no wonder that your boredom will send you into mindless wanderings.

Students need to be actively involved in the topic from the very beginning. As a way of beginning a unit or lesson, a good starting point is essential. It is vital to begin in a way that stimulates interest in your students to entice them to want to delve into the topic. This is the beginning of establishing "Serendipity Moments" in your classroom. While planning and especially carrying out the launchers, CONNECT with your students...this will show you the interests of your class and where your lesson can take you. Launching your lessons can be accomplished in many ways.

Here are some ideas for introducing new topics and lessons.

1. Literature selections

2. DVD/Video

3. Role playing

4. Intriguing item/Grab bag of unknown object

5. Food

6. Art/Poster

7. Puzzles/Riddles/Games

8. Music/Sounds

The following collection of ideas is for beginning lessons. The authors have used their combined 60 years of experience to create and compile examples in each of the above categories.

Using Literature

"March 25, 1944

It was a terrible time through which I was living. The war raged about us, and nobody knew whether or not he would be alive the next hour. My parents, brothers, sisters, and I made our home in the city, but we expected that we either would be evacuated or have to escape in some other way. By day the sound of cannon and rifle shots was almost continuous, and the nights were mysteriously filled with sparks and sudden explosions that seemed to come from some unknown depth.

I cannot describe it; I don't remember that tumult quite clearly, but I do know that all day long I was in the grip of fear. My parents tried everything to calm me, but it didn't help. I felt nothing, nothing but fear; I could neither eat nor sleep – fear clawed at my mind and body and shook me. That lasted for about a week; then came an evening and a night which I recall as though it had been yesterday" (*Anne Frank's Tales From the Secret Annex,* 1994).

Using excerpts, such as the one above, is a great way to begin a social studies class on World War II. Creating interest through Anne Frank's own words stimulates an emotional response as well as provoking thought. Through carefully selected passages from a book the teacher is whetting students' appetites to read and learn more about the topic. This type of launcher may engage reluctant readers in a fictional book or may stimulate students to research other topics related to your classroom content. Either way, your students are excited and actively engaged in the learning process.

To begin a science unit on volcanoes for elementary students, you could begin with a mythological story from Hawaii.

"The goddess Pele was the goddess of the volcano. She made fire and lava come from the volcano so that the Hog Man would not take her from her home. Now, according to the myth, Pele lives at the peak of the mountain and takes care of all the volcanoes in Hawaii. People tell this story of the goddess Pele to explain the amazing natural power and unpredictability of volcanoes" (Straner and White, 2001).

Not only does this use a different kind of literature, mythology, but it creates an exciting story to tell your students. This in turn stimulates interest for the students to want to discover more about volcanoes as well as explore more about the literature.

To introduce multiplication to second graders, Carl Sandburg can come to your aid! He wrote a poem, *Arithmetic,* where he has fun with words and numbers which can be shared with students:

"...If you take a number and double it and double it again and then double it a few more times, the number gets bigger and bigger and goes higher and higher and only arithmetic can tell you what the number is when you decide to quit doubling.

Arithmetic is where you have to multiply – and you carry the multiplication table in your head and hope you won't lose it…"

After reading the above selection, you can begin instruction with manipulative objects to demonstrate what "doubling" is which is a great way to simplify the concept of multiplying. The idea is to have fun with your students, drawing them in to learning how to multiply!

 **Using Media Selections**

Just as in literature where the teacher can make use of part or whole selections to launch a topic, DVD's and videos can be utilized the same way. An example of how to begin a study of the Revolutionary War is to show the exciting undercurrents that led to the Boston Tea Party using selected parts of the movie *Johnny Tremain*. Why might a teacher open this way? Just to fill time? Not at all; the teacher would be creating high interest to offer some understanding of why the Boston Tea Party took place so that students would be anxious to read to find answers to fulfill their further curiosities.

The Magic School Bus series offers opportunities to explore various subjects such as the earth's core. This uses a cartoon-like presentation to introduce real topics of interest. How much more fun is this avenue as compared to a textbook introduction telling the students to turn to page 23 and read the next paragraph? Not only does this avenue give the possibility for rich discussion of the topic, but it can also lend itself to unlimited possibilities such as journaling and group sharing which could lead to projects. So, hop aboard and take a ride to the center of the earth!

NOTE: Other multimedia launchers can also be utilized such as podcasts from CNN which brings daily news to students. This could enhance a study such as government or another country. Additionally, using internet sources such as United Streaming and Brain Pop can also enhance many lessons in all content areas.

Using Drama

What could be more thrilling than having Alexander Graham Bell pay a visit to your classroom? It is possible, you know, through the discovery of role-play. Two students could introduce a study on inventors and their discoveries by dramatizing the first phone call with Bell and his assistant. This could be done by the teacher writing a skit from factual information for the students to use.

As an alternative method of approaching drama, the teacher could also role-play a character from history or literature to introduce a topic of study. The teacher's goal would be to establish a specific era of time and emotion through the presentation. Therefore, some costuming would be beneficial and maybe some props for the skit to bring it to life.

A dramatization could be one of the students' most memorable and meaningful activities in the classroom community. It may be a catalyst for information later as the child progresses through school. Do you have memories of events during your school days when a teacher created an event of impact? These are things that bring curriculum alive and stay with you for a lifetime.

Using Intriguing Items

To begin, the teacher says something similar to this:

...I pulled and pulled on the line. Little did I know that I was about to reel in an unexpected surprise. I had never been deep sea fishing before, and I wasn't sure I would ever go again. But, I had an adventure I would never forget. My excursion gave me one of my most looked at and talked about pieces in my possession. Who would have ever thought that I would pull in...THIS!

At this point the teacher would pull out a shark's jaw which usually gets a reaction from the students. Questions erupt from the classroom. Where did you get that? What is that? Cool!!! That's a shark's jaw!

This opening could be used to begin a science unit on ocean life, a creative writing project, a new read aloud book, or any number of other activities. The main thing is you have created interest in your students about the upcoming activity. This kind of lesson launcher lends itself to using all kinds of possible items such as other realia (real objects). These objects may pertain to your topic to serve as an introduction. Examples are as follows:

- geography - an object, like a rock, from a particular area

- history – maybe a confederate or union cap

- mathematics – a cone, triangular prism, or oatmeal box

- fantasy story – a wand or sword

As a variation of using an intriguing item, an unknown object could be placed in a grab bag. Volunteer students could come and put their hand in the bag and feel and try to guess what it is. The teacher has carefully selected the item so that it would be related to the topic being introduced. This is promoting curiosity towards the discovery of the mystery in the bag.

High School Teachers: Don't be afraid to jump in and explore with the rest of us. Most of these suggestions can also be used in high school classes to launch a lesson in any subject.

 ## Using Food

The teacher presents a tray of beautiful pastries and asks the class, "Can you tell me the name of this food item?" The teacher prompts the students until the name, Benet, is revealed. Questioning continues as students try to identify the country where the food originates. Once the country, France, has been identified, the pastry is passed out for everyone to enjoy and "taste France" as the teacher introduces what will be studied in the next unit.

Food could introduce any other country to enable students to experience different cultures interactively. You could also use food to introduce measurement for baking, learning about the science of food, and agriculture instead of only reading or hearing about them. But, BEWARE: FOOD ALLERGIES COME TO SCHOOL!

Also, with nutrition and obesity concerns, it is wise to keep the food introductions to a minimum.

Using Art and Posters

Art can open up a world of communication. An art sample can be used to stimulate the senses for launching an exciting journey into a piece of literature, a history lesson, a geography session, or a creative writing adventure with a famous artist. For instance, Van Gogh's *Irises* could introduce either the study of plants, Holland, or encourage creative writing. Visuals are often the ticket to opening up our minds to new and exciting ventures. Keep in mind that students respond better to visual stimuli. This helps us realize the importance of showing instead of telling.

Just like an artist's artwork can serve to arouse curiosity, so can posters consisting of photographs, cartoons, factual information, math concepts, or book covers. A poster of actual pyramids can help students imagine what life would have been like during the ancient times of Egypt. This could inspire conversations about ancient kings and rulers and how the Egyptians lived and built the pyramids by hand. Hopefully, this will fuel their creative energy to want to research other related topics.

Another use of posters could be to relay factual information about a topic. An example would be geometric figures. In beginning a unit on geometry, depending on the grade level, your students would need some background about shapes and figures. This poster could give new information. It could also be used as a review of prior knowledge to transition into a new topic of geometry.

So, don't ever throw away those hidden treasures in the attic. You never know when they might launch a new exciting topic of study!

Puzzles, Riddles, and Games

"Penny's parents had three kids. One was named Nickel, and one was named Dime. What was the name of their third kid?" (Brumbaugh, Brumbaugh, and Rock, 2001)

First grade teachers could use this riddle as a way to begin a unit on denominations of coins. Students would have fun guessing the answer to the riddle without realizing they were setting themselves up for a math adventure. After a short time, the teacher would guide them to understanding the riddle through illustrations on the board supplying the correct answer if necessary.

Older students could use the following riddle to introduce critical thinking skills…(oh sorry…did you want to know the answer to the first one? It was Penny!) "An adult weighing 80 kilograms and two children, each weighing 40 kilograms, want to cross a river. Any of the three is able to row the one boat they have. The boat can hold only 80 kilograms on any one trip. How many trips will it take to get all three across a river? Remember that one trip is one time across the river, in either direction" (Brumbaugh, Brumbaugh, and Rock, 2001).

The teacher would then facilitate the thought process showing the students how to think through the problem to its solution. This launching activity will lead to further cooperative learning groups to solve other like problems demonstrating their understanding of the critical thinking skills.

For the solution to the problem, write your authors. No, just kidding…here it is:

Trip 1	Two Kids Cross
Trip 2	One Kid Returns
Trip 3	Adult Crosses
Trip 4	Kid Returns
Trip 5	Two Kids Cross

Puzzles and riddles are similar in concept in that you are looking for a solution to a problem. What child doesn't love to solve a mystery! Have you considered the thought that puzzles are actually mysteries? There are different kinds of puzzles. The most common puzzle is the literal physical puzzle (pieces that form a picture). An example of a way to use a picture puzzle would be in a kindergarten class. The teacher would have part of a puzzle put together on the floor with the children circled around it. Children would help place missing pieces in the correct places to form the picture of a farm. This puzzle could introduce the concept and vocabulary of farm life as they discuss the completed puzzle. Now the teacher is set to go on with the farm unit.

Another type of puzzle is the thinking puzzle. To introduce an American history unit on presidents you could use the following: "The 22nd and 24th presidents of the United States had the same mother and the same father, but were not brothers. How could this be so?" (Sloane and MacHale, 1993) Interesting, huh? Your students will have fun with this one. We'll let them fill you in on the answer. Okay, we'll go there. The 22nd and the 24th presidents were the same person. Grover Cleveland served two terms, but they were not in succession.

All children love to play games. Snake Eyes is a game that reinforces addition and a great way to introduce mental math. To launch your lesson try using the following: "The winner is the first person to score 100 points by rolling the dice. It is not as easy as it sounds, because there is a dangerous snake waiting to steal all of your points every time you roll the dice! Play the game in pairs using a pair of dice.

1. Each person should have a sheet of paper with their name on it.

2. Roll the dice to see who goes first. Then each player takes turns rolling the dice.

3. On your turn, roll the dice and find the sum of the top numbers. You can quit and write down that total or you can roll again. As you continue rolling the dice, keep a running total in your head. When you decide to quit, add that total to your score on your sheet of paper.

4. You can keep rolling as long as you want, but if a 1 comes up on one of the dice, you lose all your points for that turn. If two 1's come up (snake eyes), you lose all your points for the whole game and must start over again at 0!

The first person to score 100 or more points is the winner" (Blum, 1995).

Don't you think that your students will have fun not only playing the game, but also getting in to the value of mental math? As you begin using puzzles, riddles, and games with your students, you will begin to generate some of your own as a way of introducing a topic.

Music and Sounds

Similar to identifying intriguing items is the discovery of what a certain sound is. Students love to unlock the unknown.

Set the mood for anticipation. Turn out the lights for concentration of the coming sound. Tell students to listen to find out if they can figure out what they hear which will be a sound they have not heard in the classroom. "See if you can guess what it is." While the room is quiet, they listen. Coming from a tape recorder, they hear the sound of footsteps on a marble floor in a large room with a high ceiling. Additionally, they hear a bubbling fountain. Some students might recognize these sounds, but others may not realize their source at all. Therefore, questioning and prompting may be needed to guide them to the identification of the sounds of a large museum. Remember, letting them guess what they are hearing is half the fun! The teacher may need to give clues to help students figure out the source. After a short time, the teacher would reveal or confirm the identity of the sounds. This discovery should open up curiosity and imagination, as they begin to wonder what this museum has to do with the two sets of footsteps (one sounds like a pair of low-heeled shoes and the other is the sound of squeaky tennis shoes)…And why the fountain? They are preparing themselves for the adventure in the museum with Claudia and her little brother in the book, *From the Mixed-up Files of Mrs. Basil E. Frankweiler.* Hopefully, the sounds they have heard have alerted their senses and now they are ready for their reading adventure. (By the way, teachers have a way of being quite resourceful to create these sounds on the tape recorder. Knowing the excitement it can stimulate among the boys and girls can be well worth the effort!)

Similarly, music can launch activities such as creative writing where students can describe their favorite place. The teacher plays a CD of music and sounds that students respond to. In their discussion they are describing what they have heard which were crashing waves and sea gulls on the beach. As the teacher describes her own favorite place, she asks the students to consider what their favorite place is for the writing activity. Background music can be played to stimulate their minds during their writing time. After setting the stage, students should be ready to create their masterpiece.

This is by no means a complete list of lesson launchers. However, these may generate other ideas from you to accompany your specific lesson plans. Another purpose for using lesson launchers may be to review content already covered in addition to transitioning from one topic to another. As you plan, you should be thinking of the selected standards for each lesson or unit which is essential to keep in mind before you select your Lesson Launcher. As you choose your standard that you plan to teach, ask yourself, "What is the most effective way for me to begin this lesson so that my students will become curious and excited about learning?" When your idea comes, GO FOR IT, and then look and listen as students respond – directing the journey you will take.

The Connection Factor:

Promoting Excitement from the Very Beginning

Chapter 3
Differentiating with Ability Levels

Many teachers may ask, "How in the world am I going to reach each child in my classroom when they are all on different ability levels?" Well, let's tackle that question. It's true that in any given classroom there can be any number of ability levels and learning styles with your students. All students will not learn the same way or at the same speed. Some students will grasp concepts very quickly, and others will struggle with understanding the concept. Therefore, it becomes vitally important that you differentiate your curriculum and instruction so that you are meeting the needs of all your students, and so that all students are mastering important skills. Reaching each child is a challenge that must be met.

No Child Left Behind has created for us guidelines that have made teaching seem like it is an overwhelming task that is virtually impossible to handle. However, it is workable. If we remember that "one size does not fit all", then we are on our way to making progress. There are no two children that learn exactly the same way, and there are no two children that are exactly alike. What is an enriched environment for one is not necessarily an enriched environment for another.

You may ask, "What is differentiated curriculum?" Differentiation is instruction that meets the needs of the students in your classroom by offering a variety of different activities and using different learning strategies which are matched to each individual child. This means that we need to offer students a variety of different activities so they can be successful. All students will not be auditory learners. Some students are visual learners, and some students learn better by working hands-on with an activity.

There are four ways, according to Carol Ann Tomlinson (1999), that teachers can differentiate curriculum and instruction.

Content – what the students need to learn or how the students will get access to the information,

Process – activities in which the students engage in order to make sense of or master the content,

Products – culminating projects that ask the students to rehearse, apply, and extend what they have learned in a unit,

Learning environment – the way the classroom works and feels.

> *Listed in the appendix are some ways for teachers to differentiate each of those areas. Most of the examples will be geared to the elementary level; however, each can be adjusted for middle school or high school level students.*

Research has shown us that the more actively involved students are with learning, the more students are going to remember. Listed below are some reasons (Theroux, 2004) why we need to differentiate the curriculum for our students.

1. Not all students need to be doing the same thing at the same time. Some group work would therefore be appropriate.

2. Students are not all at the same level of ability and they do not learn in the same way. It follows that different groups within the same class should be working at a variety of different levels of complexity and/or difficulty simultaneously, but at different rates.

3. Students need to be actively involved in making decisions and modifications to their learning efforts.

4. Students need appropriate challenges, a secure environment, and an opportunity to explore ideas and have fun learning.

5. Students need to learn to ask questions, think and interact verbally.

6. Students need to be able to construct meaning by interacting with peers, problems, issues and with materials.

7. Learning is more effective if concepts are learned in context and related to existing knowledge. Content needs to be relevant, integrating multiple aspects simultaneously.

8. Peer teaching may be as valuable for the child who is "teaching" as for the "learner".

"A differentiated classroom offers a variety of learning options designed to tap into different reading levels, interest, and learning profiles. In a differentiated class, the teacher uses

• a variety of ways for students to explore curriculum content,

• a variety of sense-making activities or processes through which students can come to understand and 'own' information and ideas,

• a variety of options through which students can demonstrate or exhibit what they have learned" (Tomlinson, 1995).

Also, according to Tomlinson, the content in the curriculum must be carefully evaluated to provide appropriateness for learners. Tomlinson identifies key areas that are necessary to consider as ways for differentiating curriculum.

Enrichment – Enriching is going deeper and wider for those gifted and high achieving students. It extends the regular curriculum into related areas not covered by class learners.

What activities can a teacher provide for students who finish quickly and have demonstrated understanding of the lesson skill? In a third grade math class, students are expected to determine whether angles are greater than 90 degrees or less than 90 degrees. For those who quickly accomplish this task, an activity in a learning center would be helpful. After all, there is no reason for these students to do more of the same. Why not have these students measure the angles and determine exactly what degrees they are? After they have measured the angles, they can draw some of their own and have other students measure them for practice. Students generally enjoy evaluating each other, particularly when it involves their own created assessments for their peers. So, give them that opportunity!

Interdisciplinary approach – This approach integrates two or more curricular areas of study such as reading and science. For instance, select an exciting story that tells about weather phenomena. After capturing their interest with the story, you are ready to combine this information with the teaching of a science weather unit where students research different weather conditions and their effects on human life. Often when they've been motivated with a story such as this, they are ready to learn more about the subject.

Thematic Approach – Imagine how exciting history could be when it is wrapped with hands-on activities and special projects. That's what can happen when everything is focused on a central theme in a group of lessons or a unit of study such as the Civil War. Wouldn't your students love to have a conversation with Abraham Lincoln through role play? Many boys love to play with toy soldiers. How awesome would it be for them to recreate a battle scene? Create your own activities and have a blast combining imagination with facts.

Real World Connection – Kids are people too. They need to experience the real world whenever possible. Yes, it takes a lot of effort, but having a mock election during an election year is worth the time because it gives students the opportunity to actually participate in the process of being an American citizen. This is far more meaningful than simply reading about it. This connects learning to real life.

So, how can teachers appropriately differentiate curriculum for all levels of learners in their classroom and keep their sanity intact? Let's approach that and find out. Here are several instructional strategies that have proven to be beneficial in aiding teachers in accomplishing this task.

Instructional Strategies For Differentiation

Compacting the Curriculum –The gifted and high achieving students often do not need all material "taught" to them. Compacting the curriculum refers to closely uniting and condensing the material for them. For example, a teacher working with small math groups based on ability would set up the classroom so that instruction takes place in the small groups. By doing so, the teacher is allowing for differences in each group's ability as well as the activities for skill mastery. The teacher may be teaching decimals in math and when he/she works with the high ability group would compact the curriculum by teaching decimals, fractions, and percents together by showing how they are related. This way of instructing keeps these students challenged and moving forward (preventing boredom as well) while other students who are struggling would be working at their ability level and at their own pace. The teacher compacts a large amount of information into a smaller, workable piece for those who think on a higher level and don't need all the basic details.

Flexible Skills Grouping – Much as the above ability grouping, flexible skills grouping is similar with the exception being that the groups change according to skill. How in the world do you determine what skill level your students are on, and what to do about it once you know you have many levels to address? This particular instructional strategy demonstrates why pretesting skills is so important in your classroom. You MUST know where your students' strengths and weaknesses are so that you are meeting their needs on a daily basis. Using assessment data to plan your instruction is what we mean by differentiating instruction! For instance, in your math groups, a student may have difficulty with decimals, but find geometry very exciting and easy to do. Because of the student's geometry ability, he/she would be placed in a high math group for that study. Not only is the teacher differentiating effectively, but he/she is also allowing each student in her class to excel and be successful in school. A teacher who makes the effort to flexibly group students according to their skill ability is demonstrating best practices in using assessment data to drive their instruction.

Interest/Learning Centers – Centers in the classroom can be set up in various ways. The way one would approach this arrangement needs to be comfortable and manageable for the individual teacher and students. Some teachers can manage several centers, and some teachers cannot. That's okay! Finding what fits is what is important.

Words, Words, Words! All students need practice with vocabulary. To aid in this practice, a center is much more appealing than a book or worksheet. A great gift for centers is old games you may have at home or in your classroom. Use them! Something as old as Scrabble can be a real hit in a learning center. Using words from a story or other content material, a teacher would place the words in the learning center. Students would be directed to play Scrabble using the vocabulary words. To differentiate for ability, the low achievers would work with basic vocabulary words while the higher achievers would have more challenging skills such as defining the words after using them in the game.

Most kids love science. Think about making a science learning center. To assist students in choosing their activity for the center, you could color code in regards to ability level. Students would know in advance the appropriate color to help them in choosing the task. The teacher has planned the tasks in order to differentiate for each group. In a plant study, the low achievers and/or English Language Learners could be required to draw a picture of the plant model in this center and identify the parts by labeling their illustration. Average ability students could be required to draw and label the plant parts as well as explain the function of each part. Your high achievers could be given examples of different kinds of vegetation in different geographical locations (such as cacti vs. tropical plants) and analyze the difference between them based on location, temperature, and other variables. Remember…to differentiate successfully, every group needs learning experiences at their level. By doing this, the success rate of your centers will improve.

Not only are centers good for elementary students, but they could also be used at the middle and high school levels as well. The teacher prepares learning stations where students practice skills previously taught or perform other activities related to subject matter. Even older students enjoy and benefit from moving around!

Tips for finding space for centers:

- student desks arranged in square or circle
- tables in classroom
- corners or floor space to accommodate small groups
- teacher desktop
- DON'T FORGET: a computer activity can be a center

Tiered Assignments – In tiered lessons, "the content is presented at varying levels of complexity, but the process is the same for all students" (Adams and Pierce, 2003). Tomlinson (1999) states that "a tiered lesson addresses a particular standard, key concept, and generalization, but allows several pathways for students to arrive at an understanding of these components. Lessons can be tiered according to students' readiness (ability to understand a particular level of content), learning profiles (styles of learning), or interests (student interest in the topics to be studied)."

Even though this may seem challenging at first, the process of creating your own tiered lessons boils down to a few essential steps

(Adams and Pierce, 2003).

1.   Identify the standard (national, state, district) that you are targeting.

2.   Identify the key concept and generalization. The key concept follows from the standard, and the generalization follows from the concept. Ask yourself, "What big idea am I targeting?" and "What do I want the students to know at the end of the lesson?"

3.   Assess whether students have the background necessary to be successful in the lesson. Ask, "What must have already been covered or what must the students have already learned?"

4.   Select what you will tier – content, process, or product.

5.   Decide how you will tier – student readiness, interest, or learning profile.

6.   Determine how many tiers you will need and develop the lesson.

When students are doing group work, there still needs to be some clearly defined structure within the classroom. Having anchoring activities such as brainteasers and puzzles for those who finish quickly will help. "Anchoring activities promote 'What's next?' thinking - rather than the attitude 'I'm done!'" (Adams and Pierce, 2003).

Independent Projects – This strategy embraces the concept of differentiation to the max. Students work independently on projects of interest which are geared to their ability level. This also enables students to work at their own pace completing the work within a given time frame. Think back to your childhood. What project meant the most to you? Which one gave you the most opportunity to show your personality? Which one presented the best learning experience? Teachers, don't hold back on this one. Project topics can be anything from inventors to flying machines to space exploration and beyond.

Use your own creativity as a catalyst for your students and let their imaginations soar!

Higher Order Thinking – Within the framework of your classroom curriculum, it is important for you, as the teacher, to remember to challenge your students to think at higher levels. Using Bloom's Hierarchy of Thinking enables your students to learn to think and progress from the concrete to the abstract. While progress has been made in the teaching of critical thinking, there are still times when much of the classroom discussion only requires students to think at the knowledge and comprehension levels. As you plan your lessons keep in mind the need for students to develop higher order thinking skills. Try to include activities that enable students to apply principles, rules, and facts instead of simply recalling them. As students become more capable thinkers, they will begin to analyze and evaluate information.

The following information will help you in creating questions and activities to aid your students in learning to think at higher levels. As you see below, your goal is to get your students evaluating (the highest order of thinking) and not just recalling information (the most basic order of thinking).

Benjamin Bloom's Hierarchy of Thinking

Evaluation – Development of Opinions, Judgments or Decisions
Do you agree or disagree and why?
What do you think about _____?
What is the most important _____ and why?
What criteria would you use to assess _____?

Synthesis – Combination of Ideas to Form a New Whole
What would you predict/infer from _____?
How would you create/design a new _____?

What might happen if you combined _____ with _____?
What if I eliminated a part?
What if I reversed or rearranged?
What solutions would you suggest for _____?

Analysis – Separation of a Whole into Component Parts
Classify _____ according to _____.
Outline/Diagram/Web
How does _____ compare/contrast with _____?
What evidence can you present for _____?

Application – Use of Facts, Rules, Principles
How is _____ an example of _____?
How is _____ related to _____?

Comprehension – Organization and Selection of Facts and Ideas
Retell (in your own words)
What is the main idea of _____?

Knowledge – Identification and Recall of Information
Who, What, When, Where, How, Describe, List

The time has come for us to prepare our future citizens to problem solve. This should not be left to only your gifted and high achieving students. Every child, no matter what ability level, needs to be challenged. RAISE THE BAR....You might be pleasantly surprised as you allow Serendipity to transpire!

Now that we have shared some instructional strategies for differentiating curriculum for your students, we hope that you find some comfort in knowing that others struggle with this as well. If you do not have a grasp on the rationale behind differentiating curriculum and instruction, then it certainly can become a daunting task. However, it is doable within your classroom when you find what works for you and your students.

Importantly, remember that differentiation is not more of something; rather, it is doing something differently. Don't be afraid to try new approaches according to your students' needs. These approaches may just be the ticket to your students' success.

The Connection Factor:
Finding What Works to Meet Student Needs

Chapter Four
Considering Language Differences

This chapter contains information and ideas for instruction using best practices in today's educational arena. Therefore, the instructional strategies discussed are not only helpful to those who are teaching English Language Learners, but should also offer ideas for teaching in all circumstances.

Now that we have discussed the topic of how to teach various ability levels, let's look at tactics teachers can use to teach students who are learning English, often simultaneously with other content. Depending on the effect of the influx of immigrants in specific parts of the United States, the education scene has been met with an enor-

mous challenge that has affected classroom teachers and special education teachers, along with results in school testing and school an-
nual yearly progress reports. That challenge has been how to go about
teaching students who speak other native languages and are limited
in English. In the last couple of decades much has progressively been
learned with many strides made in this field. We will only scratch the
surface here. Hopefully, by simplifying the subject as best we can,
teachers who have not been trained in the field of teaching speakers
of other languages can find in this chapter, concepts and/or strategies
to aid in their teaching English Language Learners (ELL's) to learn
more successfully.

It is vital to remember that these students come to classrooms
not only with different language levels (level of no or very limited
English, beginning level, and intermediate level), but also with diverse cultures, educational backgrounds, and yes, they too enter our
classes with different ability levels! Yikes! How do we reach all students with so many complex issues without taking away from those
who are "ready to take off"? That's where we are reminded that the
strategies for differentiating instruction, which were discussed in the
previous chapter, can apply here also. The discussion that follows is
an attempt to aid in your understanding how to specifically help students who need to learn or improve their English comprehension and
usage as they are working side by side with your other students.

The first step is to recognize that these students who have little or no English proficiency are like all other students in that they
feel and think according to their baseline of prior experiences and
knowledge. What makes them the absolute same as all children is
that they have not only a desire, but also a need to feel comfortable
and safe in their classrooms. Some have entered the U.S. from war-
torn countries, longtime family separation, or extreme poverty all
of which gives them reason to be fearful or tense within their new
environment. Even those who have come from stable backgrounds
will find that attending a school with an unfamiliar language can be
downright scary. Without the assurance of safety and comfort, there

is little chance of reaching them.

How can you begin giving these students confidence? It's as simple as a smile! This is particularly true for those non-English speakers with whom you cannot yet verbally communicate. There's a saying that goes something like this: "Smiles are the same in all languages." That expression and gesture of kindness, used as often as possible, can actually be your first form of successful communication. It's as if you're saying to the student, "It's going to be okay." Your first line of business is to keep reassuring beginning ELL's because they are in a stressful state during this time when they do not comprehend what's going on. They may or may not display their feelings, but this uncertainty can be upsetting to them. Some go home to release their stress with tears that they have hidden during the school day. If they receive positive reassurance from their teacher, they are going to gain more and more self-assurance which will aid in relieving their stress and make room for learning.

Secondly, what you and they must accept is that learning another language is not an overnight undertaking. These students learn language at different speeds just as native English speakers learn at different speeds and just as all students have strengths and weaknesses of all kinds. Some find math easy, for instance, and some are good athletes or musicians while others are not. Let's take into account that some will find learning language easy while some will not. So, patience is the virtue we're looking for here!

Next, teachers who set up their classrooms with a family atmosphere, no matter what age or grade, will add to the comfort level. (Won't this hold true for all students?) Offering other students the opportunity to be a part of assuring the beginning ELL, as much as possible, will help all concerned. It feels good to the learner when someone cares enough to lend a helping hand, but it also can add a measure of confidence and fulfillment to those who help. Indeed, if possible, it's beneficial to the new arrival, a limited English student, to first have a bilingual classmate (if available) to orient the new student to the classroom and content for a certain period of time. However, use caution here as this assistance must not go on for a long period of time because the bilingual student - and the native language itself - will become a crutch and will hamper the ELL in learning English. After all, why learn English if it is not needed?

The trick for the teacher is to use the Serendipity Principle with The Connection Factor, paying close attention to the student's needs to determine how much to use scaffolding methods, such as peer helpers and other adaptations, and when to move away from them. Some teachers may be inclined to do so too early, as in using "tough love" which could cause the student to give up and even shut down. Then other teachers might tend to be too soft, giving the student too long of a dependency period, actually hampering their English development. Since it can be rather problematic to make this call for an inexperienced teacher, experimentation to determine what is best for each individual is usu-ally best. A temporary trial is not going to hurt anything! Your goal is to determine the soonest effective time to move the student towards more independence. It's like seeing the whole picture coming together, one piece at a time.

For the classroom, Bilingual and Picture Dictionaries/Pictionaries will serve you and the student well towards better communication the first year. Some older students have their own bilingual dictionaries (or hand-held technological/electronic translators), but having a couple of extra bilingual dictionaries as references in the classroom for teacher and student use is advantageous to all. Please realize that a bilingual  dictionary is not going to help a child who did not learn to read in his/her native language. This refers to younger students who left their native country before learning to read in their native language. Also affected are older students with low educational background. Sometimes a picture that comes from anywhere: a pictionary, book, magazine, computer image, or a drawing can serve the purpose of getting a point across. And, you don't have to be an artist to get a quick thought passed from one to another, much like the Pictionary Game.

Realia (real objects) are effective items to use when available. During instruction these objects bring ideas alive and actually serve as a help for native English speakers too since all do not have the same base of prior knowledge. So, any time you use realia, you're giving a more hands-on approach which is more meaningful to all students. For instance, when you read a book, having samples of objects in the content can bring meaning to students. Sometimes just simply pointing to a picture or object will clarify a point while orally reading or talking.

Other helpful pointers to consider for better communication is using facial expressions and gestures with your hands to convey something which is much like dramatizing. Modeling language patterns and structures orally in class or when individually speaking to the language learner is the natural course of demonstrating expectations.

Ask questions to the ELL's that are appropriate to their language proficiency level. For instance, beginning learners respond better to questions that require only an action or one or two words as responses.

"For those not yet speaking, offer two choices as answers to your questions. Hold out your two hands. Point to one hand as you say one answer and the other hand for the other answer. By doing this, the teacher's goal is that the ELL will point to or touch one hand as their choice. It's a grand event when this technique works as you realize you're connecting and opening up communication! Often ELL's will have more of a receptive language than you may realize when they are not yet verbalizing" (Threlkeld, 2008).

The intermediate or the more advanced learner may need open-ended questions which have more than one right answer and then follow-up questions to help them extend their answers. In other words, they may succeed in giving you what you're looking for if they are prompted by you.

Remember that beginning learners tend to acquire language in meaningful "chunks". Chunks of information may have more meaning than unfamiliar isolated words and are certainly easier to digest than too much information which would be a case of overload. Think about how native English speakers in pre-school and kindergarten learn to develop language. They are learning with songs and nursery rhymes and through predictable read-aloud books with patterns, etc. As much as you, the teacher, can expose this type of teaching to the upper grade students who are learning language, you will be helping them "take in" portions of language while they are having fun doing it. This type of teaching can be carried out in a center or small-group instruction in an upper grade classroom.

In regards to communicating with parents of your ELL's, there are varied situations.

First of all, sometimes one parent speaks English pretty well. Therefore, conversing with that parent may not be a problem. There is a warning that comes with this scenario: the parent may have only a working knowledge of English and may appear/sound pretty English proficient and will indicate that they understand what you say. If you say, "Did you understand that?", you can be assured they will say that they did even if they did not! It's a pride thing. Perhaps they understood part, but not all of what you said. Or maybe they thought they understood, but indeed did not. So, you'll have to "feel this out" in time to determine their true comprehension. Some of them can even feel a little offended if you suggest an interpreter.

Next, for those parents who do not speak English well or at all, arranging translators may be necessary. If they have their own resource person, they may bring them along to a conference. If not, you may be fortunate to have a translator in your school or community to arrange for his/her assistance during a conference or to make a phone call for you.

There is another consideration regarding parents of ELL's who speak little or no English. They may not necessarily be ignoring the student's work, teacher's notes, or newsletters in English that you send home for them to read; instead, they may simply be unable to read them in English. Even if they have a family resource person to read English for them, that procedure takes time. First they have to arrange this procedure with their resource, then read through the material, and finally respond with the translator. So, your understanding of these stressful steps for them and the potential for a timely process would be a compassionate act, as opposed to quickly judging them for not quickly responding.

Tip: In papers you send home, highlight the most pertinent information for them to read and respond to, telling them of this plan beforehand. This will reduce a lot of family pressure at home for them if you help them "cut to the chase"! If there is a very important document, hopefully, a teacher can have that translated into their native language. Some school systems help with that – possibly through the English Speakers of Other Languages or Special Education Departments.

The previous discussion is a simplified way of looking at communication with beginning ELL's and their parents, particularly bearing in mind the teacher who has no working skills of the student's native language. Hopefully, the point has come across that the teacher needs to relax with the situation. Give the student time to adjust and do not stress over the lack of quality communication for a while. It will not last. You'll be amazed at what will happen with the student's language learning within the first few months. After at least a year, normally a good usage of "survival" English is intact. This early oral English is known as Basic Interpersonal Communication Skills (BICS) as determined by Canadian linguist James Cummins (1992). These language BICS are learned by daily use in social speaking situations such as playground or break talk, requiring anywhere from a few months to three years of practice for proficiency. BICS can be accompanied by beginning English reading and writing skills.

Can you see how valuable it is to include our limited-English students in various oral and social activities such as cooperative learning and interactive activities? They can learn more language from their peers than from their teacher since conversation is interactive!

Think again about how native English pre-school children learn language. They learn by hearing and speaking. So do ELL's. And, the next question is – do native English pre-schoolers speak "correctly" in the beginning stages? No, and neither do ELL's, but if English Language Learners feel free to experiment with their speech, they will progress in time. Thus, teachers should correct oral speech and beginning writing only when it is necessary for meaning during this early part of the developmental stage to aid in their feeling free to experiment. Keep in mind: the lack of listening and speaking opportunities will result in poor progress.

Moving to the higher form of processing regarding the abstract language of academics, Cummins has more to say to help us understand the difficulty of ELL's comprehension of context-embedded material. Here he identifies the other dimension of language as Cognitive Academic Language Proficiency (CALP). This dimension of language, CALP, involves language skills needed in school tasks such as taking notes on a lecture and writing a report to summarize information that was assigned to read. These CALP skills can take from five to seven years (or longer in some cases) to acquire.

To assist you in relating to CALP, just imagine that you are attending a Japanese school and after being there a year (and learning some Japanese BICS), you are assigned to read a Japanese "chapter book" on the same level as native Japanese speakers. Then, using the Japanese language, you are instructed to write a summary, critique, and/or reflection of the book. Better yet, think of studying in Russia as a sixth grader and within your first year there being assigned a social studies chapter to read in the Russian text and then take a written test on the content. We think you get the picture!

Cummins uses the clever metaphor of an iceberg to explain the relationship between BICS and CALP.

• The tip of the iceberg which can be seen above water is represented by BICS in that we can see and hear students using basic competency in communication. (First, "Bathroom" as a request then progressing to "I go bathroom?" to "Please I need go bathroom?" to "May I go to the bathroom, please?")

• But be cautious! When the student begins speaking more correctly, teachers are easily misled into thinking they are completely ready for the higher CALP skills, including being evaluated the same as native English speakers. Note: these CALP skills are necessary for the student to have success in these complex academic tasks. Since CALP (cognitive academic language proficiency) skills require more abstract processing and expression, it is important for the teacher to remember that ELL's must develop these skills, such as summarizing, critiquing, and reflecting which require deciphering through details within a great deal of terminology to find main concepts, etc. You may agree that those skills can be difficult for many native English speakers!

• Students need comprehensible input. Without help, meaning cannot be attained. Listening to an unknown language or copying unfamiliar words/sentences alone has no meaning. Supporting the ELL through this long developmental process is the role of the teacher. Each student is an individual, so methods of supporting students vary in their degree of effectiveness. If the teacher makes an effort to find successful ways to use scaffolding techniques, the ELL should succeed in time unless there are abnormalities which need to be investigated when progress does not occur. However, often this "investigation" or evaluation can be done too early within the developmental/BICS stage resulting in invalid outcomes. So, again, remember that patience is vital. Don't panic when a student is "slow" to language progress…this may not be his/her strongpoint.

• It is the CALP dimension of language that is beneath the surface of the water within the iceberg, still "unseen" during the development of language. Cognitively demanding tasks such as writing a two-page essay that an ELL is not yet ready to perform will give a teacher an invalid picture of the student's knowledge and skills. The student may know and understand certain knowledge, but cannot yet convey those thoughts in high-level English with any reliability which is why a modified assignment should be given to replace the higher skill. A modified version of the two-page essay may be to have a separate rubric to evaluate the ELL's "essay" differently than others. Simple sentences and lists of facts, for instance, may be acceptable as opposed to complex sentences within paragraph form.

• Assessing ELL's can be carried out much the same way as teaching them: modifying what you appropriately expect of them to match their language level. This is not to take away from their learning what the class is learning. The teacher's task in getting the knowledge and skills across may be different for ELL's as may the assessment of the content. Yet, as with other students, teachers need to evaluate according to what they believe is fair to expect of the ELL's. (There will be more about strategies in this chapter and assessments in Chapter Five.)

There are other significant points for teachers' considerations in terms of ELL's learning our language:

• Students who enter a United States school who have received a good basic educational background in their native language stand a far better chance of progressing in a second language and succeeding in school in general than those who do not have a strong educational background in their native language. This is due to their prior knowledge in one language being transferred to another. Additionally, because they have spent some time learning content and skills in their previous schools, it is probable that they will fit into the academic world in your classroom successfully in due time. Obviously, those with the lesser educational background will need more extensive adaptations in order to thrive in their learning.

• Just keep in mind that lack of education and language does not necessarily mean lack of intelligence. If you make a deliberate point to seek out ways to tap into a student's ability, you may be pleasantly surprised to find evidence of intelligence. Most of us will agree that all children can learn.

• The piece of the preceding statement that is missing is all children learn *differently.* If that is true of native English speakers, it is certainly true of students learning English as a second language as well.

• Additionally, there is the position that if a student has a strong native language usage intact, he can better transfer his language knowledge to a second language as opposed to those students whose native language has been interrupted. An example of this interruption would be a child – adopted from another country – who had begun the language of that country and then moved to the U.S. to be "thrown" into a new language at only age 3 or 4 when he was unable to get far with his first language. This interruption can cause some confusion with some ELL's. This scenario also commonly occurs with children born in the USA who stayed at home with mom and only learned their family native language. These children begin Pre-K with no English and begin learning English with their first language underdeveloped. Some handle this language developmental interruption fine; others do not.

• Since a more complete development of the first language is ideal, a teacher should never discourage a family from continuing to use their native language at home. Not only will speaking the native language at home help the younger student with language development, preventing complete interruption of the native language, but the older student can better express higher order thinking in his/her native language until CALP in English has been more fully developed.

In the previous discussion, the aim has been to set the foundation for teachers who have not been fully trained to teach English Language Learners to get a better grip on the reasons certain suggestions will be given. If you understand the typical characteristics and issues of students learning a new language, you'll hopefully be more effective in carrying out ways to help them learn both our language and other subject content. In other words, the instructional methods to aid an ELL's learning more effectively that are forthcoming should make more sense to you if certain understandings are in place. Normally if we understand why, we can go forward with what and how.

 Before considering various strategies, there is an important matter to clarify in order for instructional strategies to be effective - teachers should be apparent in their appreciation of students' cultures. Rather than our having a chapter on cultures, we will simply give an important tip about that topic: read about and study the culture of your ELL's background country and/or culture. This may be in regards to their country from which they came, but it could also be their parents' former country/culture in the event the student did not live there or was too young to remember living there. Consider that sometimes there are mixed cultures in terms of two parents from two different countries/cultures.

Obviously, books and the internet can serve as helpful resources for teachers. When ELL students see that their teacher is making the effort to learn about their cultures, this will really "light them up"! Their classmates will also enjoy learning the similarities and differences in their cultures as a comparison and contrast to ours. Having children's literature and artifacts available from the "other countries" for children to explore will add to the dimension of learning and appreciating other cultures. This connection will help build relationships with you, your ELL students, and the entire class. This understanding of their lives will enable you "...to increase the relevance of lessons and make examples more meaningful" (Burnette, 1999).

Strategies for Teaching English Language Learners

Here are instructional strategies suggested by Jane Burnette (1999):

- **Use a variety of instructional strategies and learning activities**. Variety will provide students with opportunities to learn in ways that are responsive to their own communication styles, cognitive styles, and aptitudes. Variety will help them to develop and strengthen other approaches to learning.

- **Consider language skills** when developing learning objectives and instructional activities.

- **Incorporate objectives for affective and personal development**. Provide opportunities for high- and low- achievers to boost their self-esteem, develop positive self-attributes, and enhance their strengths and talents which can enhance motivation to learn and achieve.

- **Communicate expectations.** It may be necessary to encourage students who expect to achieve mastery, but are struggling to do so. They may need to know that they have the ability to achieve mastery, but must work through the difficulty.

  "If students know your expectations, it will give them a goal to work towards. The more information you can give students towards expectations, the better chance there is for quality work as a result. Giving them a rubric before a project, for instance, will help them understand how you plan to evaluate. Many will perform on a higher level when this information is clarified for them early on" (Threlkeld, 2008).

- **Provide rationales** by explaining (or giving them a certain understanding of) the benefits of learning a concept, skill, or task. Help them see the application to their lives.

- **Use advance- and post- organizers.** At the beginning of lessons, give the students an overview and tell them the purpose or goal of the activity. If applicable, tell the order that the lesson will follow and relate it to previous lessons. At the end of the lesson, summarize its main points.

- **Provide frequent reviews of the content learned.** For example, check with the students to see if they remember the difference between simple and compound sentences. Provide a brief review of the previous lesson before continuing on to a new and related lesson.

- **Facilitate independence in thinking and action.** When teachers ask students to evaluate their own work or progress, they are facilitating independence. Asking them to perform for the class, such as reciting or role-playing, promotes independence.

- **Promote student on-task behavior** which maintains a high level of intensity of instruction. By starting lessons promptly and minimizing transition time between lessons, teachers can help students stay on task. Shifting smoothly (no halts) and efficiently (no wasted effort) from one lesson to another and being business like about housekeeping tasks such as handing out papers and setting up audiovisual equipment helps to maintain their attention. Keeping students actively involved in the lessons (for example, by asking questions that require students to recall information or solve problems) also helps them to stay focused and increases the intensity of instruction.

- **Monitor students' academic progress during lessons and independent work.** Check with students to see if they need assistance before they have to ask for help.

"This will assure that they are on the right track before they begin doing the task incorrectly. Besides, they usually will want to 'save face' and not ask too many questions in front of their peers" (Threlkeld, 2008).

• **Provide frequent feedback** which is preferred at multiple levels. For example, acknowledging a correct response is a form of brief feedback, while prompting a student who has given an incorrect answer by providing clues or repeating or rephrasing the question is another level. The teacher may also give positive feedback by stating the appropriate aspects of a student's performance. Finally, the teacher may give positive corrective feedback by making students aware of specific aspects of their performance that need work, reviewing concepts and asking questions, making suggestions for improvement, and having the students correct their work.

• **Require mastery** of one task before going to another. When mastery is achieved on one aspect or portion of the task, give students corrective feedback to let them know what aspects they have mastered and what aspects still need more work. After the task is complete, let the student know that the mastery was reached.

So far, have we shared any approach that would not benefit *all* students? Many techniques that are suggested for English Language Learners can benefit many (or even *all*) students as they are normally overall good teaching methods. Hopefully, you will find that position to be valid as you continue thinking about our further suggestions.

More Strategies

Teaching the Text Backwards

A very valuable technique that can benefit all students (including ELL's) is to reverse the traditional sequence for teaching textbook-based material which is now known as "teaching the text backwards" (Jameson, 2004). You may remember the traditional sequence of procedures as follows:

1. Read the text.

2. Answer the study questions.

3. Discuss the material in class.

4. Do selected applications based on the material.

This above traditional sequence is very difficult for students limited in English as it is for those who have difficulty reading "dry text". The ELL's may not have prior knowledge to apply to reading. Additionally, the material may be embedded with difficult terminology. The sequence for teaching the textbook "backwards" is more effective:

1. Do selected applications based on the material.

2. Discuss the material in class.

3. Answer the study questions at the end of the chapter.

4. Read the text.

Can you see that by beginning with a **hands-on activity** (possibly with a partner, group or class) the material will be more meaningful and will come alive for English Language Learners when they "experience" with others to fulfill their task? The activity will aid in their understanding of concepts and vocabulary to follow. This increases comprehension by putting the new material in context.

• One example of an application based on the material to introduce the text is a field trip for the entire class to participate in, early in the unit, rather than at the end. This will enable the rest of the unit to have more meaning after first experiencing the topic.

• Another prototype is to interview families about what countries their ancestors came from before starting a unit on immigration or geography. Look how much more meaning the unit will have when it is studied!

• In a basic computer class, before students learn relevant terminology or practice keyboard skills, a teacher could "struggle" with preparing a simple document dramatizing the difficulty of attempting to do the task with unknown skills. This order of events will give them purpose and motivation for learning computer skills after they "witness" the need.

Now you can comprehend how much more meaningful it would be to be able to discuss something you have already experienced! Don't we all like to talk about what we know rather than what we do not know?

Asking students to review by **answering study questions** at the end of the chapter to identify main ideas after the hands-on activities and discussion set a purpose for the reading assignment that will follow which makes more sense! Finally, when students read, the text now has a far better chance of all coming together as it gels due to already experiencing much of the text. These students who are learning English along with other students who struggle with reading comprehension will more easily **read with understanding.**

This order of events makes more sense to any student. To further aid in understanding, teachers can assign the reading by breaking up the chapter to reduce the amount of text each student reads. This technique should increase comprehension and model study skills. Graphic organizers and visuals can be used to demonstrate key relationships in the content and increase comprehensibility and thinking skills.

The previous discussion served to demonstrate how teachers can implement principles of increasing comprehensibility, increasing interaction, and increasing thinking and study skills where much of the learning occurs through textbook-based material. This Teaching the Text Backwards method aids both ELL's and other students who are less skilled in reading or who learn best through less traditional learning styles. "It is a practical, consistent framework for teaching and learning into which additional ELL strategies can be integrated" (Jameson, 2004).

Will the gifted and high-achieving students suffer with the application of this technique of Teaching the Text Backwards? No. In fact, they will also enjoy this way of learning so that gaining knowledge will become more concrete and meaningful, leaving time and room to surpass the basic, giving those students the opportunity to excel. While the teacher is helping the students who need more assistance in learning the basic content, the gifted students will have time to soar to areas of their interests.

Graphic Organizers

The application of graphic organizers is not a brand new concept, but these aids have "caught on fire" in the past decade as teachers of all levels (elementary through college) have realized their positive effect on learning. In 1984, Novak and Gowin discovered that using these teaching tools enhance learning in the following ways:

- By reducing verbal text and increasing focus on key concepts and vocabulary
- By broadening thinking skills
- By simplifying learning

"Various objectives can occur while exposing students to the organization of thinking through graphics such as presenting concepts of cause-effect, problem-solution, comparison-contrast, sequencing, sorting, note-taking skills, focusing attention during instruction, showing relationships, keeping the flow of ideas moving, quickening reading as it filters through details, presenting a method of assistance towards recalling facts due to fewer words (to enhance memory skills), and linking ideas. They serve as advantages for visual learners and as a way of exhibiting checklists. They can serve as semantic mapping to help give language meaning and can present research findings in a clear-cut way. They fight boredom as teachers instruct and put all students on equal ground as they participate in brainstorming activities. These organizers or word maps can also serve as study guides and as pre-writing skills.

Many teachers may not have discovered that these tools can also provide a way of assessing. For instance, the class has studied ancient Egyptians. As many students take a typical chapter test or write paragraphs to answer questions, the ELL's (and some special education students) who are not yet ready to perform on the high test-taking level, can fill out a blank graphic organizer such as a T-Chart listing with words or pictures on the left side of the T – the foods the Egyptians ate and on the right side – their inventions. The students will have demonstrated their understanding of the goals of the unit by revealing what they do know, rather than what they do not know. After all, if the ELL students are not yet into their CALP dimension of language, how can they realistically respond to the high vocabulary questions? They may even be able to read a lot of the words in the questions and directions of a test, but if only one word is misunderstood, they may not be able to respond to the question or topic correctly. Would that give a teacher a valid evaluation of their knowledge on this topic? Think about it" (Threlkeld, 2008).

Here are some examples of graphic organizers/visuals/word maps:

- Brainstorming Web

- Chart

- Graph

- KWHL Chart (what we know, what we want to know, how can we find out, what did we learn?)

- Venn Diagram – to demonstrate comparison/contrast

- Thinking Grid – to check column to answer question in categories

- Matrix – a template with rows/ Ex: columns to compare characteristics of animals

- Flowchart – showing relationships or sequencing

For ideas about graphic aids and others, there are many websites some of which are the following:

www.graphic.org
www.fno.org/oct97/grids.html
www.cast.org/publications/ncac/ncac_go.html
www.education-world.com/a_lesson
OR—just Google graphic organizers!

Cooperative Learning

Research has shown that cooperative learning improves students' academic achievement, social skills, and self-esteem (Johnson, Johnson, & Holobec, 1991).

As already discussed in this book, people (young and old) learn more effectively when they are brainstorming with other people. We've also pointed out the importance of children learning to work together to prepare them for a better future in the working world. With these points in mind, there are a few ideas we will share with you on ways to incorporate techniques for students to work together.

Whenever possible, chunks of language and new knowledge can be utilized into **activities and spontaneous games**. You can adapt these games according to levels of students (both language and ability levels) and the entire class can enjoy learning together.

"An example of such a game is 'Trash Ball' which can be a 2-team activity where the teacher can control the questions (simple to difficult) according to whose turn it is and can ask questions that match the student. The designated student may elect to have the team help with answers which must be given in a timely manner. If the answer is given correctly, a point is given to that team and the student attempts a bonus point by throwing the ball into the empty trashcan propped up on a chair or table. All ages love this game as it appeals to most due to the ball-throwing component and often becomes quite exciting. The students who feel they need help with questions have the option of legitimately turning to peers for assistance which promotes team spirit. Most of them choose the assistance because they don't want to individually lose a point for their team which gets them off the hook. It's all about learning, not evaluating or peer pressure. Tip: This game serves well as an open-book review of a Social Studies or Science unit or chapter prior to a test" (Threlkeld, 2008).

Group Projects are excellent ways to have students work and learn together. Normally, if the task is to produce a finished product such as research facts, puzzle, mural with a story, dramatic skit, or book, students enjoy having a joint purpose. There is more success if the group has been instructed and given ample time to cooperatively plan, use manipulative materials, synthesize ideas, possibly research, and put it all together in a way that promotes pride. The more students participate in these types of activities, the more they will learn to plan and work together successfully as a group. The teacher's role is to set up these groups thoughtfully and give guidance as to individual roles of the students. There are many things for teachers to consider: dividing groups differently each time, planning for materials needed for student access, modeling and discussing expectations of group behavior, finding ways to motivate students towards genuine collaborative efforts, and providing a group rubric for evaluation.

Think, Pair, and Share (TPS) is a way of helping all students to collaborate in pairs:

1. Think individually first about a given topic.

2. Talk about the ideas with a partner.

3. Share ideas that came out of the "pair talk" with the entire class or large group.

Another version of TPS is the **One-Minute Paper** where students, in response to a given topic, write or draw for one minute. Then partners can read each other's paper and finally share significant points of their partner's paper with the entire class.

Total Physical Response (TPR)

TPR is a strategy which can introduce new language using body movement. Remember "Hokey Pokey", "Head, Shoulder, Knees and Toes", and "Simon Says"? These are examples of ways to combine movement and vocabulary which help the student to remember what he/she is learning. It is true that a teacher of 2nd – 3rd grade and up may find it challenging to include TPR activities as a part of the classroom schedule on a regular basis, but it can be done when the teacher thinks creatively.

Consider that when teaching a history lesson about a ship taking explorers across the sea, the entire class would benefit from a ship ride with the teacher as the captain giving out orders! The ELL's order could be as simple as "Bring me your compass", while others can have problems or questions presented to them such as "Point in the direction of Italy as we leave Greece" or "Which country do you think we'll come to next?" (Threlkeld, 2008)

As you can see, Total Physical Response can benefit all students of all ages. We all need movement – and fun!

Jigsaw Activity

Students are divided into home teams by the teacher. Each member leaves that home team to temporarily become a member of another group – a study team with a topic to read, research, and discuss main points while taking notes. After doing so, they now have become an expert on that topic. After the study tasks are completed by all study teams, each go back to their home teams to report findings. In essence, they are teaching to their home team. An ELL who is capable of taking notes in the first group, then going back to read or share findings with their home team, would feel on top of the world to be considered an "expert" on a new topic. After all, he/she will know more than anyone in the home team about that new information! This activity should boost egos of all participants.

Gallery Walk

Students work together in small groups to answer a question or solve a problem. They are instructed to create an artifact such as a chart, graphic organizer, illustration, model, or experiment. After completion of artifacts, the results are displayed around the room and student groups rotate to view the artifacts. Students leave written feedback by the artifacts; Post-It notes work well for this feedback activity. Students learn by creating and also by critically viewing other groups' work. ELL's often successfully participate in all aspects of this activity.

There are many more ideas for teaching English Language Learners within the classroom: puppetry, drama, role-play, pantomiming, listening/media centers, dancing, labeling, and on and on. It's all about helping the students relate to the language. Find a way to connect with the ELL's and they may just surprise you — even beyond your imagination!

The Connection Factor: Cultivating Opportunities for Language Growth

Chapter Five
Assessing

In keeping with our theme of serendipity, we have found that what we have learned through the years pertaining to assessing is based on our serendipitous moments - finding what works and what does not. Therefore, as we share the following, know that what we are reporting to you is pulled from both research and personal teaching experiences. Maybe we can save you some headaches and give you some shortcuts as to what works best! Also, our aim is to give you a clear overall view of this important topic.

Tests, tests, tests…Is anyone sick of that topic? It may be that the true concept of evaluation or assessment may be misunderstood because what should be the true meaning or purpose has been lost in the shuffle. In some form, assessing and evaluating is a necessity, but there haven't been many people, children or adults, who react positively to the idea of being evaluated when something is at stake. Think of when you were a student and how nervous it made you feel…Will the questions that are asked be about topics I have studied?

Will I be able to think clearly? Will I fail or make a good grade/score on the test? Even confident, brilliant students can be "tricked" on a test if questions or problems are worded obscurely.

And then there are the high-stakes standardized tests, which most all would agree are simply cruel…cruel to students, cruel to parents, and cruel to teachers and schools because of the undue pressure and anxiety these tests put on everyone. The unfairness to students is attributed to their sitting down to a test which determines their promotion or retention, which in itself could paralyze their thinking process. While there certainly is a place for standardized testing (to serve as a part of the whole picture of a student's achievement), it is the obsession concerning the test results that concerns us. In fact, aside from the tremendous cost of testing each student year after year, who really believes that anyone can be evaluated on one given day (or a series of days) with much validity regarding what a student knows? Therein lies the key to this chapter:

In our view, the main **purpose of assessing** should be to aid in **making instructional decisions.** We believe in planning for student assessment and recommend that teachers aim to determine the following when assessing:

- What students know and can do

- What their weaknesses are

- How they process learning

- What progress has been made

- Where to go from there

Our source for the following quoted and cited information on the topic of standardized testing comes from Carole Cox's textbook, *Teaching Language Arts: A Student-Centered Classroom* (2008). In her text, she quotes:

"Standardized tests are based on a behaviorist model, which describes learning as a set of subskills that can be separately taught, mastered, and tested. Multiple-choice tests reflect this model of learning. They can pinpoint what skill a student has difficulty with and make a reliable comparison of his or her ability with that of other students. But these types of tests cannot explain what went wrong in the process. Moreover they are not aligned with or instructionally sensitive to state, district, or school standards and curriculum and therefore do not provide information on whether the goals of standards-based programs have been met" (Tierney, Johnston, Moore, & Valencia, 2000).

"This has been particularly true in lower-performing schools, where more time has reportedly been spent on test preparation, than in higher-performing schools" (Hoffman, Assaf, Pennington, & Paris, 2001). Furthermore, an interesting ironic thought is shared by Hoffman, Assaf, Pennington and Paris concerning this point in that spending time on meaningful instruction may be more critical in lower-performing schools, which may also have specific goals and standards for progress that require more time to meet. So, we say, where is the sense in spending so much test prep time?

The position of the International Reading Association (IRA) in 1999 on the issue of high-stakes assessment and literacy was as follows:

> The International Reading Association strongly opposes high-stakes testing. Alarmingly, U.S. policy makers and educators are increasingly relying on single test scores to make important decisions about students. For example, if a student receives a high score on one high-stakes test, it could place him in an honors class or a gifted program. On the other hand, if a student receives a low score on

one test, she could be rejected by a particular college. These tests can also be used to influence teachers' salaries, or rate a school district in comparison with others.

The Association believes that important conceptual, practical, and ethical issues must be considered by those who are responsible for designing and implementing test programs. Assessment should be used to improve instruction and benefit students rather than compare and pigeonhole them.

We would like to state that it is our understanding that more and more states are addressing the issue of aligning standards and curriculum, therefore making testing more relevant to content. In that regard, there may be improvements on the horizon considering the actual standardized test items matching what students are doing in the classroom. However, in view of what the IRA said above, "Assessment should be used to improve instruction and benefit students rather than compare and pigeonhole them", we have chosen the essence of this chapter to focus upon authentic assessment discussed below. (Also as you read further in this chapter, we will clarify something you may not have thought much about - that there is a difference in "assessment" and "evaluation".)

Now let's move towards classroom assessment that should be authentic. Again, we will apply Carole Cox's information from the formerly mentioned text to describe the attributes of **authentic assessment:**

- Information is gathered by teachers and students.

- Ongoing, daily observations are made.

- Multiple sources of information are used.

- Information is considered in the context of process.

- Artifacts (writing, art, journals, and tapes) and rich descriptions (anecdotal records, checklists) are used.

- Teachers and students make decisions about assessment.

- Information is gathered as part of the classroom schedule.

The results of assessments should be the driving force behind your plan for instruction. This would be why using the same detailed lesson plans year after year is a thing of the past since the above statement would be unable to be applied! If you find that a group of students (or even a single individual) needs to work on a particular skill, plan your instruction accordingly. Keep in mind too, that if a few students have obtained this skill, they should not be subjected to being "retaught" and drilled on this skill that they have already successfully demonstrated. Instead, they can work on another skill (or possibly a higher-order thinking task related to that same skill) while you're helping those who need more instruction. Remember the Differentiation Chapter? That's the message there: teach what needs to be taught to those who need the instruction....just a reminder!

We previously established clearly and emphatically that students learn differently. Therefore, they also should have varied opportunities to demonstrate their acquired knowledge and skills. In other words, they can also be assessed differently. According to Robert Marzano (2000), who has been a researcher with Mid-continent Research for Education and Learning, there are seven basic forms of classroom assessment that may be used in almost any classroom setting. These are shown on the next page.

Seven Forms of Assessment

Robert Marzano

Form of Assessment	Characteristics
1. Forced-choice	* multiple choice, matching, true/false, fill-in-the blank * can be scored objectively * most common form of assessment * choose from among alternatives given
2. Essay	* good for assessing thinking and reasoning skills * opportunity to demonstrate knowledge of relationships * gives information on how students process knowledge * scoring can be subjective
3. Short written responses	* mini-essays * brief explanations of information or processes * scoring more objective than for essays
4. Oral reports	* assess student speaking ability * similar to essay, but more impromptu * require acute listening skills to score
5. Teacher observation	* informal * best for process-oriented and nonachievement factors * good when linked to interview * teacher notes used to record observation results
6. Student self-assessment	* most underused form of assessment * helps develop higher-order metacognitive skills * assessment conference allows student to clarify own level of learning
7. Performance tasks	* requires students to construct responses, apply knowledge * require more than recall of information * can assess a variety of forms of knowledge and skills * scoring dependent on tasks

Involving students in assessing their own learning helps them to understand their performance relating to the established expectations. Students can be given the opportunity to self-assess and reflect upon an assigned topic. This enables students to evaluate their own work. For instance, they can record their thoughts in a learning log. Periodically, the teacher has the option to hold a conference with the student to discuss the log. This interaction helps the student clarify their level of learning which would include their strengths and weaknesses regarding the pertinent concepts and skills. The teacher's goal is to help students develop metacognitive skills. Afterall, evaluating information is the highest level of thinking within Bloom's Hierarchy of Thinking.

The teacher can pick and choose what assessment form is best for each task or standard and in the case of the need to be diversified in assessing differently for different students, a teacher may choose assorted assessments for a given standard. If you are not an experienced teacher (relative to authentic assessments), you will learn to match types of assessments to the appropriate time to use them. This comes with practice.

An effective way to put different types of assessments together to build an overview of learning is through the use of a **portfolio** which is a popular assessment tool. Teachers and students assemble artifacts to represent evidence of student learning based upon established criteria within a rubric. The idea is to see growth in each student's learning which normally promotes pride in students, parents, and teachers. It is also an easy way to spot weaknesses to help the teacher see where the student needs to improve. An example of this is in expressive writing. If a writing sample is contributed to the portfolio once a week to show "work in progress", the teacher can check to see if a particular skill has been achieved or not. This "silent evaluation" drives the teacher's plan for instruction. If this student (and possibly others), for example, is having difficulty with possessive plurals, the teacher will plan instruction in the form of a mini-lesson on this topic for those who need it as a result of that finding.

Backward Design (Wiggins and McTighe, 1998) is a concept linking curriculum, instruction, and assessment in meaningful ways. It is a unique, interconnected approach to planning for teaching and learning. The first decision is to determine desired learning results from the curriculum. Next, the teacher identifies how to collect the evidence necessary to know if the results have been achieved (assessment). Finally, the last step is to choose how to help students acquire the desired knowledge and skills (instruction).

To recap the 3 steps of Backward Design:

- Select desired curriculum results from particular standards.
- Collect evidence to demonstrate degree of achievement which is assessing.
- Plan instruction according to findings.

So, is assessment always going after a grade? NO. The above method of planning instruction demonstrates a method of pre-testing before teaching a unit of study which, of course, would not be graded. Now, about that necessary **assigning of grades**...let's approach that topic. Evaluating achievement after standards have been taught is indeed necessary and purposeful.

It may help to discuss the **difference in assessing and evaluating** for a grade. According to Sara Davis Powell (2009) in her textbook, *An Introduction to Education: Choosing Your Teaching Path,* assessment is gathering evidence of student learning (step 2 of backward design). Evaluation makes judgments about, and assigns value to, the results of assessments. It is not necessary, nor advisable, to evaluate all evidence of student learning. For instance, a teacher may assess note-taking skills of a student by checking on the completeness and organization of note cards the student filled out during research (the first formative assessment). This gives the teacher feedback in order to help the student make corrections in the research process and then move forward with the project. This is simply a matter of - did this student complete this important first step completely and correctly? Since this procedure falls under the category of observation, a record of the step being satisfactorily achieved with a check in a grade book may be all that is necessary. If a teacher prefers to have more of a rating system – such as a number scale from 1-4 - regarding a degree of satisfactory performance, that assessment method would also suffice for simple record-keeping sake. Evaluations for grades are not needed during work in progress. The end result of the project would be the time to assign a grade. Hopefully, this example of assessment during the research process (before final evaluation grade) illuminates how assessment and evaluation differ.

When the above project is first assigned, a student needs to know the expectations of the teacher so that he/she can work towards fulfilling those expectations satisfactorily. These expectations can be shown clearly in a **rubric**, a tool to help make subjective evaluation more consistent. In the appendix (D), we have provided an example of a rubric. Along with that rubric, a conversion – converting scores to grades – can also be provided early on for the student. The conversion might be as follows:

- A total score of 17-20 would earn an A
- 13-16 = B
- 9-12 = C
- 7-8= D
- 1-6 = F.

If a student knows exactly what it takes to make his or her desired grade, it is likely that he/she will work towards that goal. These work goals may be compared to an adult who will work for the pay he needs or wants. Another way of looking at work ethics is having a desire to work towards a quality outcome due to pride. No matter how you cut it, some students have a greater desire to succeed than others. Your job as teacher is to inspire the others who lack pride!

When teaching content, a teacher should help students see the **big picture** by assisting them in filtering through the details to get to the main ideas. This is a skill that was generally not taught very well years ago. Instead, students were encouraged to memorize meaningless material for tests and then they walked away from these tests with little retention or understanding of the knowledge. In other words, it is not important exactly when World War II was fought if you don't have an understanding as to why. We authors have noticed throughout our own personal teaching careers that in the last one to two decades it has become apparent that this important skill needs to be taught to students so that they take away the big picture. Teachers ought to keep in mind the need for students to acquire this important skill. Therefore, to help students acquire this ability, focus on ways to accomplish this while planning, instructing, and assessing. Teachers are learning valuable techniques to help them carry out this goal.

One effective method is teaching and evaluating with graphic organizers. First, the teacher teaches using a **graphic organizer** (for the purpose of modeling - guiding students through information to identify the main idea), then the blank organizer can later serve as an evaluation tool (as discussed in Chapter Four). This method can help the student obtain and retain the main idea. It is easier to remember one main idea (and a few related details) than it is to retain all of the many details that accompany that concept. If you can help your students learn how to determine the big ideas of the topic of study, you will have served them well.

Closure to lessons is obviously important to help students understand content that has been taught - in relation to acquiring the big picture. This is the time to wrap up the loose ends and thoughts about the topic in order to bring cohesiveness to the study. This brief conclusion will not only help the students' comprehension, but also will help the teacher assess whether or not the goals were met. As the teacher reflects about the students' performance regarding the goals of the lesson, it is important to note which students did not get the basic idea and which students are ready to move on.

Let's go to a second grade classroom where students have been learning to use money as a medium of exchange. The **big idea and core task** of the standard taught was for students to identify denominations of money and be able to find the sum of a set of coins and currency. As the teacher is closing this instruction and practice time, he or she should assess to distinguish as to whether or not each student has been successful in performing this skill. Small group instruction may be needed for those students who have not mastered this skill.

For those students who have demonstrated the understanding of the basics of the above standard, they may begin working on a higher skill that is **important to know and do**. For instance, the next step could be for students to count back change and use decimal notation and the dollar and cent symbols to represent a collection of coins and currency. While these students are working with partners counting back change, the teacher can be reteaching the core task to those students who are struggling. Remember our discussion on meeting the needs of all students? With good planning, you can have students working on different tasks and skills. This is one way this can be done.

Through quality teacher observation, a means of assessing, the teacher can identify those students who need a higher challenge. These students could work in a small group to produce a basic book-keeping system. They could create a way of showing deposits, expenditures, and balance to experience this life skill. There are some gifted second grade students who need the experience and opportunity to work toward a higher goal. The rest of the class will benefit from this shared information that is **worth being familiar with**.

Below you will find a graphic showing the **clarification of content priorities** to simplify the previous discussion. Wiggins and McTighe (2004) in *Understanding by Design* have created a way for teachers to work through massive amounts of content to show what tasks are fundamental and necessary in order to perform other tasks.

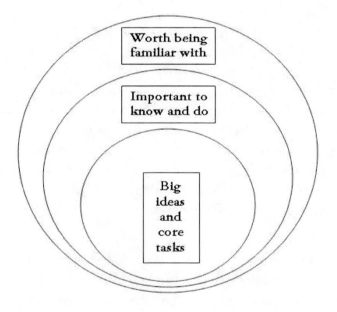

Clarifying Content Priorities
G.P. Wiggins and J. McTighe

Worth being familiar with

Important to know and do

Big ideas and core tasks

Today's respected assessment expert, W. James Popham, stated at an assessment conference in 2003, "It would be my honor and, frankly, my pleasure to lead an uprising against how this nation currently tests its students."

In his speech, "If I Were America's Assessment Czar", Popham declared three assessment decrees, one of which is the following:

"Any test used for purposes of education accountability
must also be instructionally supportive."

So, there you have it!

The assessment discussion in this chapter has been about discovering what works for your students. Testing should not stifle imaginative teaching. Rather it should be a positive influence to help you plan as you connect with your students to help them succeed.

Assessing that drives instruction is a demonstration of utilizing The Connection Factor and can take you to a level of teaching that is extraordinary.

The Connection Factor: Plugging in to Your Students to Assess Their Needs

Chapter Six
Unfolding the Plan

To tie together much of what we have already discussed, let's develop a mini-unit to show the cognitive process of planning a unit – going from point A to point B through the completion of a mini-unit. First, we will clarify the differences between the various types of lessons and units. Consider the age and interests of your students in planning the following:

- Mini-lesson – brief 5-10 minute lesson on a specific skill

- Lesson – 15-45 minutes, usually covered in one day

- Mini-unit – 3-5 days for a topic study

- Unit – 2 weeks or longer for a more extensive topic study

We have chosen to develop a mini-unit for a fifth-eighth grade class since these ages and grade levels would be more of a midpoint. Teachers should be able to adjust accordingly, up or down, by following our plan.

The starting point will always be based on what you want to accomplish within your lesson or unit. We have chosen to use the Fifth Grade-Eighth Grade National Education Standards for Social Studies and Language Arts for our focus. These standards are easily found on the Internet. When selecting standards, don't forget that how you teach them is where your individual teaching creativity comes in. Don't forget to have some fun with your planning so it will follow through in your teaching!

Step One: What is the focus of the lesson?

U.S. Constitution Mini-Unit

I. Identify Standards

A. All Students

NSS-C.5-8.3 PRINCIPLES OF DEMOCRACY

How Does the Government Established by the Constitution Embody the Purposes, Values, and Principles of American Democracy?

• How are power and responsibility distributed, shared, and limited in the government established by the United States Constitution?
• What does the national government do?

• How are state and local governments organized and what do they do?

• Who represents you in local, state, and national governments?

• What is the place of law in the American constitutional system?

• How does the American political system provide for choice and opportunities for participation?

NL-ENG.K-12.1 READING FOR PERSPECTIVE

Students read a wide range of print and nonprint texts to build an understanding of texts, of themselves, and of the cultures of the United States and the world; to acquire new information; to respond to the needs and demands of society and the workplace; and for personal fulfillment. Among these texts are fiction and nonfiction, classic and contemporary works.

NL-ENG.K-12.4 COMMUNICATION SKILLS

Students adjust their use of spoken, written, and visual language (e.g., conventions, style, vocabulary) to communicate effectively with a variety of audiences and for different purposes.

NL-ENG.K-12.6 APPLYING KNOWLEDGE

Students apply knowledge of language structure, language conventions (e.g., spelling and punctuation), media techniques, figurative language, and genre to create, critique, and discuss print and nonprint texts.

NL-ENG.K-12.8 DEVELOPING RESEARCH SKILLS

Students use a variety of technological and information resources (e.g., libraries, databases, computer networks, video) to gather and synthesize information and to create and communicate knowledge.

NL-ENG.K-12.12 APPLYING LANGUAGE SKILLS

Students use spoken, written, and visual language to accomplish their own purposes (e.g., for learning, enjoyment, persuasion, and the exchange of information).

I. B.   Modification for English Language Learners

NL-ENG.K-12.10 APPLYING NON-ENGLISH PERSPECTIVES

Students whose first language is not English make use of their first language to develop competency in the English language arts and to develop understanding of content across the curriculum.

II. Lesson Launcher for mini-unit

Step Two: Where do I begin?

Our goal for the mini-unit is to help the students understand how our government works through our Constitution. Our goal for the lesson launcher is for students to see the need for a Constitution while encouraging them to want to know more. This is the point where you "reel them in" with interest and excitement!

To begin the study on the Constitution, ask students to respond to the following question: What do you think life would be like in a country where there were no laws or rules specifying the way we should behave or live? You may want them to consider how their actions (such as stealing from one another) would affect others if there were no limits in a society. As a form of brainstorming, have your students respond individually in writing before any discussion takes place.

After ample time has been given for their response, discuss with students their ideas about living in a world without limits. Help them see how chaotic their environment would be without some kind of order. This brainstorming and discussion should bring together points for understanding the need for an established Constitution.

As a pre-assessment for the U.S. CONSTITUTION MINI-UNIT, have the students complete a brief "survey" to gather their base knowledge of the Legislative, Executive, and Judicial Branches, along with the States and Amendment process. The result can serve as a guide for the teacher to group students into their research groups. This will enable students to research information in which they show evidence of a lack of knowledge.

III. Mini-unit Activities

Day One: Preamble Activity with Technology - As a whole class activity, the teacher leads research through an appropriate website designed to learn about the Constitution. Within the website, www.usconstitution.net, the teacher can demonstrate interactively how they can learn more about the Preamble by clicking onto links available within the document. In this way, the class has an opportunity to explore together various terms and interesting facts and explanations about the Constitution concentrating on the Preamble. An example would be the word "defence" which

> **Step Three: Unfolding the plan - How can research be fun and inviting?**

is used as a link. When you click here, you will find an interesting page about misspellings in the U.S. Constitution. They will learn that words have changed in the spelling and meaning since 1787. As Mount (2008) explains in this site, many words were written in the British form (such as defence, labour, and controul) since the American spelling of words was inconsistent at best. Another example that can be found on this site is clicking the word Preamble, then the word "Note". This takes you to an extensive page with concise explanations of each phrase of the Preamble. This would help the students understand the terminology, thus helping them clarify this part of the document to make it more meaningful. This interactive website gives a broad introduction to the Constitution and zeroes in on information of curiosity and interest.

We suggest three methods of carrying out this technology activity:

• The teacher could lead the instruction using a computer projector with students participating through discussion and possibly coming up to the computer with the teacher to choose links for the class to read and discuss.

• The above equipment is not always readily available. An alternative to using a projection system is for the teacher to invite students to join the teacher at his/her computer, making room for students to sit in a semi-circle around the computer so that it is visible to all. Of course, space must be allotted for this. This procedure may work for 5th- 6th graders and lower, but may not be advisable for older students.

• Finally, another procedure for this technology activity is to carry it out in a computer lab with the teacher leading students to the website and links.

Day Two: Cooperative Learning Research – Students will be working in cooperative learning groups in the technology lab on this day for their research on the Constitution. It is advisable to identify learning groups and your expectations for their work before going to the technology lab. This will encourage students to get settled and begin working quickly. Students should already know that they will continue to work on the previously mentioned website.

> **While keeping the standards in mind, how can I allow for student choice?**

With that in mind, a teacher could divide the research in this way:

- Group 1 – Legislative Branch
- Group 2 – Executive Branch
- Group 3 – Judicial Branch
- Group 4 – The States
- Group 5 – Amendment Process

The students will know that their expectations will be to collect information about their topic to share as a group with the rest of the class (to be planned the next day). They will make preparations for their project based on the expectations in the Group Presentation Rubric which each student will have received. This rubric will aid them in gathering information and completing the assigned project in the following days. See Rubric Sample in Appendix D.

Day Three: Further Research and Planning - Student groups will continue research if it is needed. However, the main focus of the day will be on planning their presentation for the rest of the class. The teacher will facilitate these plans by floating from group to group and assisting where needed. The teacher should encourage the students to use their creativity in preparing their presentation so that they can capture the interest of their classmates while sharing their information. Students are encouraged to use drama, art, music, and other components to produce an interesting and thought provoking presentation. Before finalization of plans, each group should have the teacher's final stamp of approval for their presentation.

Day Four: Finalize Plans and Rehearse Presentation – Students will be given time to complete their projects and then rehearse their presentation for the next day.

Day Five: Group Presentations – The teacher uses a Group Presentation Rubric to evaluate each group. Also the teacher helps students reveal pertinent information on each topic through discussion for closure and clarification.

> **Day Five is where you will find those "serendipitous moments". Look for them!**

The teacher will use his/her discretion as to whether the rubric serves as a sufficient assessment for the unit or if a more formal assessment is also needed.

We would like to point out two things about this mini-unit we have shared with you as a demonstration of how to develop a plan:

Notice that we purposefully developed a plan to demonstrate students taking ownership for their learning which is why we chose to include cooperative learning activities in this mini-unit. Our experience tells us that when students buy in to their own learning, the outcome is better because they learn and retain more. Think about it, don't you perform better when you have choices and some open reins as to where you can go with your choices? Students are the same in that they can get excited when they have been given the opportunity to gather knowledge and prepare ways to share it creatively. Remember, not only are they learning by researching the information, but also the entire class is gaining knowledge from classmates' shared presentations.

We have included the sample of a rubric (see Appendix D) to emphasize a point. If the rubric is shared as a way of letting students know what the expectations are before they begin their project, then the teacher should see better quality work as a result. Most students will work more diligently towards specific goals rather than vague ones. We know; we've tried it both ways! Make your expectations clear and help students stay on track with those goals by monitoring closely what they're doing, and you will be amazed at what they will learn from the experience!

Just as teachers help guide students to reach goals, teachers also need to make a conscientious effort to achieve instructional goals while planning!

Practice What You Preach!

The Connection Factor: Planning Well to Maximize Prospects for Serendipity!

Chapter Seven
Serendipity Stories

The best way to demonstrate and help you visualize how serendipity teaching works is to give actual examples. This chapter will share real teachers' real stories. Please notice that each teacher who reveals their special serendipity moment gives us an example of what can happen when we consider students' interests, curiosities, and needs. Keep in mind that the stories are only a small part of the actual lesson or situation and may not include what the teacher may have used as his/her standard for the lesson, the lesson launcher, or any differentiation strategy that may have taken place. Our main purpose in sharing the stories is twofold: to demonstrate how teachers connect with students and to inspire others to seek those serendipitous moments during instruction.

Grandmother's Visit

In my sixth grade language arts classroom, I felt that I needed to give my students an experience with a non-fiction novel. We had previously enjoyed many good fiction authors, but I knew it was time to teach them the appreciation of historical people whose lives would be of interest to them as sixth graders. This exposure would help them learn characteristics of non-fiction and how it contrasts with fiction. My book choice to read aloud to the students was the biography of Helen Keller. My goal was to introduce to them the joy of reading about real people and understanding the elements of nonfiction.

As we got into the story, reading a chapter or two a day, I noticed the students had become enthralled with this fascinating woman and her accomplishments, especially when considering her tremendous obstacles. After completing the book, it was apparent that more on this subject was desired by them. As we discussed their amazement of living and learning successfully as a person who was blind and deaf, one student, Renee, shared that her grandmother had always been blind and had to overcome this difficulty in her life. Again the students' curiosity perked up after hearing this. I could have said, "Thank you for sharing that," and moved on to something else as teachers often do, but something inside me knew this topic of Renee's grandmother should be explored. I think this was apparent because Renee was so proud of her grandmother and I recognized this. I said, "Do you think she would like to visit us and let us ask her questions about living with blindness?" She was thrilled at this prospect, telling me that she knew her grandmother would be honored. Plans were made for the visit. When her grandmother visited, the students were polite and respectful and asked appropriate questions because of what they had already learned through Helen Keller's life story.

After the visit, not only did the students write thank-you notes stating their respect for her accomplishments, but many of them also wanted to learn Braille – on their own. Those students interested in this activity set up a station, and when they had the opportunity to go to the station and practice, they totally were involved in this new venture!

Now I will admit, learning Braille was not a performance standard in our system, but who's going to put out a fire when it comes to having fun with learning? Non-fiction characteristics and letter-writing skills, however, were on the required sixth grade checklist of knowledge and skills to be learned. In other words, learning more than the required standards is certainly okay and can be a load of fun as demonstrated by these students who took pride in making Braille pamphlets!

I conclude that because I listened and responded to Renee, we did not miss out on these special learning moments.

Beth Threlkeld, sixth grade teacher

Disney Still Magical

I teach in a Middle School in a self-contained classroom for students within the Autism Spectrum Disorder. Most of the curriculum is based on vocational, social and personal management skills to prepare these wonderful students for life after school and to teach them to be as independent as possible. Functional academics are also an important skill that is typically taught individually or in a small group setting (1 adult to 2 to 3 students) because of their poor attention span. Often times my students have a very hard time staying focused and do not enjoy a good "challenge". They like structure and the expected. When introducing a new skill, this can really throw them for a loop!

Children with autism generally are best taught using visual techniques. My biggest challenge as a teacher is to teach them to want to initiate socialization and actually enjoy it. For many years, my class has had a "social skills" lesson on a daily basis. One day, I was trying to play a game of UNO (the regular deck of UNO cards) with the boys (my students are usually boys) and they were fighting me every step of the way. Some were insisting to leave the table while others were simply looking away and definitely not focusing on the task at hand. I wondered how I would get them to initiate any type of "play" with each other if I could not even get them to play a game with me!

After many tears and tantrums from one of the boys, I almost gave up. Instead of giving up, I went to my closet of games and decided to try one more time. I looked into the closet and found another game of Disney UNO that I had completely forgotten about. If you know anything about children with Autism, you may know that many of the students love anything with a Disney theme. I pulled out the new UNO game and decided to give it a try. I quickly dealt out the cards, hoping for some success and praying for no more meltdowns! The student that had been crying looked at the cards and started smiling. All of the cards had Disney princesses on them and he knew all of them by name. Every time it was one of the student's turns, I would ask them to sing the song from the movie of the princess card they were laying down. The boys started laughing and looking at each other. They even corrected each other and helped each other sing the songs! They played 2 games of UNO while laughing, singing and most of all, participating with enjoyment. This was too good to be true!

After this day, I wondered how I could make all aspects of learning fun for these children. I've got it! When practicing counting, use Disney characters. When learning to read, use Disney books and make worksheets with anything Disney on it and especially when teaching social skills, incorporate Disney into the conversation. This has helped many of my students tremendously.

My students will always have obstacles to overcome in their lives, but one of the keys to their success is creating a structured environment and incorporating their high interests into the curriculum. With these children we must make adaptations within ourselves and our environments to help them be successful. Additionally, when goals are difficult to meet, sometimes persistence will lead the way –

to open another door to a serendipitous moment!

Peggy Vanover, sixth, seventh, and eighth grade moderate autism class

Tech, the Ticket

My present teaching position is to instruct middle school elective classes called Careers Connections. The ultimate goal of the course is for students to obtain a jump start into their future by looking at their interests and aptitudes, and matching them to possible occupations. Each nine week grading period I am challenged with a new group of three different grade levels - sixth, seventh, and eighth graders.

The time again came to meet a new group of students for one class. As the group of 30+ eighth grade students arrived at my trailer, the usual anticipation and excitement was present for the students as well as for myself as we came together to find out what this nine weeks would bring. I can recall as students were seated on this first day that they were quiet and a bit timid as we were going over class expectations and procedures.

All were on task with the exception of one student, Lee. Lee had gray tinted glasses, was thin and very studious in his physical appearance. While I talked to the class, he made paper airplanes, drew and mumbled to himself. For a while I ignored the behavior, but then as it continued, I asked him quietly to put the airplane away. As if I had not asked for his cooperation, he ignored my request by continuing to draw. I realized instinctively that I needed to choose my battles wisely and to leave it alone at this point. This was a diverse class and having several special needs children was not uncommon. Lee's behavior seemed defiant as he appeared to be quite apathetic regarding what was transpiring in our class. I then realized it was "Lee" about whom I had received information prior to this class, but with a full day of brand new students, it did not cross my mind to look out for him in this particular class.

The statement I had been given had informed me that Lee was mildly autistic and could be mistaken for a child with a bad attitude. After the first day, we started discussing students' interests. Lee was the first one to volunteer his goals. He reported to us without hesitation that he wanted to be an engineer. In our open conversation, I responded that he must like putting things together, taking things apart, and then fixing them. He readily confirmed this and proceeded to share that he had projects he was working on at home. I asked if his mom was aware of his interests and plans. He openly verified that she was, along with the admission that he was on restriction for almost catching things on fire. Normally this statement would end with an exclamation point, but not with Lee. It was just a matter of fact statement. Still, I felt as though we were making a connection.

As a little time went by, I was pleased that Lee continued to contribute to class discussions with his expertise. I gravitated towards his interests and strengths, using them to help other students. Lee became our "peer computer tutor" and my "computer specialist". This role provided him with self-confidence, positive social interaction, and the feeling of being needed. The astonishing thing was that students accepted his oddities, such as his monotone voice and peculiar comments he would make. (If you know anything about the traits of the middle school student, this acceptance by the other students was pretty remarkable.)

All students had been given the opportunity to have their parents volunteer to be a guest speaker in our class. This is a great way to reinforce parent support with their child and the school system. Lee was the first one to return his form indicating that his mom desired to be a guest speaker. When Lee's mom arrived, she and I spoke privately about her presentation concerning being a registered nurse. She then took this opportunity to ask me how I honestly believed Lee was perceived by his classmates. She shared that her main concern was her son's social relationships. I described to her the role that I assigned him (peer computer tutor) and how it came about with his desire to be an engineer based on his aptitude. I also explained how I thought the students felt he was smart and different, but in a "cool way". Her eyes swelled with tears of joy. As she was obviously moved by this, she said, "That's exactly what I was hoping for."

I have since then realized that we never know when we can directly make an impact on a life by having an open mind and not judging a book by its cover. By enabling Lee in this class to have a positive experience, it is my sincere hope that he will fulfill his dream to be an engineer – or maybe a even a computer scientist. We certainly gave him the chance to discover that his aptitude has a place in this world and I hope others will recognize this too.

Katie Losurdo, middle school teacher

This teacher has demonstrated through her story the importance of making the effort to connect with all students – not just those who are easily approached. When The Connection Factor is in place, look where it might take you! This serendipitous time with Lee was almost miraculous as he responded to his teacher's acceptance of him and his idiosyncrasies, turning them into gifts that were perhaps unknown because they were not yet found in the school setting.

Winter Walk Adventure

It happened in the middle of a very long and cold winter after a snow fall of about two feet. We had brought snow inside to play with in our water table. We made snowflakes and learned about their six sided configurations. We had learned about the weather changes that needed to take place for snow to fall. But my wonderful class of 18 preschoolers needed to get outside and expend some energy! Of course, we had been out every day to play, making snowmen and snow women, building forts and sliding down our modest hill each time we went out. We had had a lot of fun, but we needed to do something different.

That day the sun glistened on the snow and seemed to beckon me out on to the field that was a part of the church school's property. I called to the children to follow me, and we began to explore. We decided to pretend that we were explorers in the Arctic. I called out to ask if anyone saw any "snow caps" or "mountains" as we traveled across the "terrain". When we neared the parking lot where the snow had been plowed into high mounds, I said, "Look at those mountains! Do you think we can climb them?" We all did, helping each other with the climb.

We went on to find islands and peninsulas in the parking lot. No one complained about the cold. We were on an adventure! By the time we headed inside, we knew we had launched into a wondrous discovery of the world of land formations. You can imagine the fun we had creating tunnels, exploring caves, and climbing mountains in the classroom that winter. We even had icebergs floating in our water table, each made from various frozen shapes including ice cubes. The children really got into it and their vocabulary expanded as we named, made, and played with each land form.

I've used that idea of a "winter walk adventure" on many occasions since then and it continues to be a wonder to me how much the children enjoy it. It's so simple. Just add snow and a little imagination and you never know where it might take you!

Lynn Olson Wilson, preschool teacher

Climate Check

As a middle school counselor, I picked up a technique at a QUEST inservice years ago that I found most helpful in classroom guidance, small group counseling, and individual sessions with students. I additionally utilized it with adults in various venues.

The technique I refer to is the "climate check" which is a way of checking in with someone using a simple number scale of one to ten. When I would first introduce this concept to a class, I would say something like this:

"I would like to begin this class lesson with a climate check. What I need for you to do is think of a number between one and ten that describes how you are feeling at this time with one being 'the pits', with five being 'so-so', and ten being 'on top of the world'. As we go around the room, listen for each other's climate with no comments. It is NOT about knowing why someone has a specific number, BUT about being aware that someone's day may not be going quite as well as yours. If they have a five or under, at some point in the day he/she might appreciate an extra smile or a word of encouragement."

It was powerful watching the students as they listened to each other. I kept this practice going my entire career. Students came to expect it and welcomed the opportunity to heighten awareness without going into details. I also told them the climate check gave me a better feel for how I might need to adjust the lesson. Over the years I found this to be a great way to connect with the students and to help them respect each other. I realize now that I was using the Principle of Serendipity in that we never knew where our climate check might take us. I know that opening up to the students can be a meaningful journey.

Robinn Rogers, middle school counselor

Double Duty

I have a student in my class who has an uncle who is a soldier in Iraq. She talks about him frequently and I can tell she is close to him, missing him greatly and wanting him to come home. We started studying Government (the roles of the president, governors, and mayors) in Social Studies. I integrated it into our Writing Unit of writing friendly letters. We had been working on writing friendly letters to the President that we actually planned to send to him. I stressed that these were friendly letters and we only needed to say acceptable things. This student in particular was the one I stressed this to because she was borderline gifted, and she was NOT afraid to say whatever she felt! She felt so strongly about this that I just didn't have the heart to tell her she shouldn't include her feelings in her letter. We worked on a way we could write the President and tell him nicely and persuasively that she wanted her uncle to come home from Iraq. Since she had very high ability and always worked quickly, I knew she'd finish her letter sooner than everyone else. So, I called her over and offered her the opportunity to additionally send a friendly letter to her uncle in Iraq. I told her that if she could get the address from her mom, we would send it to him and then they could become pen pals. She could then continue practicing writing friendly letters to him. I knew this would be very meaningful to her; I was right because she was SO excited about it. This was not an assignment for everyone in the class because not everyone had this situation. I did not believe that everyone would learn from this experience in the way I thought she would because it wasn't relative or meaningful for them.

It is now my thought that this occurrence served two purposes. Not only did it assist the child in coping with the anxiety she was experiencing due to her uncle being very far from home fighting in a war, but she also simultaneously was practicing to become more skilled in letter-writing. I am pleased that I tuned in to this child who was motivated to respond, applying learning in a meaningful way. Since this "assignment", which was not originally planned, was for this one appropriate child, I believe this activity for her would fall under the Serendipity Principle where the result was better than I could possibly have imagined!

Amy Rine, student teacher in second grade class

Missing Dinosaurs

Last Friday one of my Kindergartners (Quinn) lost two dinosaurs he brought to school. One was blue and the other was yellow. Both were about six inches long. They were on the shelf up above our jackets in the kindergarten hallway in the early afternoon and gone by bus time. We asked other teachers and students to help find our missing dinosaurs.

This turned out to be a great teachable moment because we talked about not bringing toys to school, and if they did (they could on show and tell days), they would need to keep them zipped up inside their backpacks. The students were also very motivated to write slogans and words asking for the dinosaurs "safe return" and worked very hard on their writing. This event inspired their writing activity and the results were much better than I ever expected.

By the way, as an outcome to this activity, the dinosaurs were returned and harmony restored!

Erik Swenson, kindergarten teacher

Miniature Investigators

This is my 12th year teaching kindergarten. Each year, it seems we expect more and more from our kindergartners. -Don't get me wrong- I, too, have high expectations in my classroom, but we often forget that some of these little guys just aren't ready. To help meet the many challenges and expectations in my classroom, I am constantly trying to find ways to make learning fun. This year, sight word study has been one of my many goals. We currently have 45 kindergarten sight words. By the end of the year, we strive to have our kindergarten students reading the sight words at a rate of 30 words per minute.

To help make learning sight words fun for my students, I used the theme of "Word Detectives." I gave each child a "mission" (a list of 3-4 sight words). They were instructed to take the word list and search in other classrooms in the school to find and read the words on their list. I dressed them up in "Spy Gear" or detective gear, equipped them with a magnifying glass, and followed them with a video camera around the school. The "spy gear" included hats, glasses, dark clothing, and even mustaches for the boys if they wanted one!

They had so much fun finding and reading the words on their list as they pretended to be detectives. We also learned two Jack Hartman songs, *The Word Detectives* and *Hop Over It*. I recorded the students singing the two songs and used the footage of the detectives searching for sight words to make a DVD for each child in my classroom.

The students LOVE the DVD because I added cool spy music to the footage of their word hunt. I also added the K-2 sight words at the end of the DVD for extra practice. I have had several parents comment on the fact that their child wants to watch the DVD over and over again. Students are learning their sight words while having fun learning. It IS possible!

Suzanne Grisham, kindergarten teacher

Because this teacher CONNECTED WITH HER STUDENTS and created an activity based on their interests, she applied the Principle of Serendipity in her planning of activities. Each success led to another.

Snowball of Kindness

One of my favorite memories of my teaching career, which spanned forty years, was Project Snowball of Kindness in a third grade class. In my classroom, I always tried to instill in my students the concepts of teamwork, respect for others, and a caring, giving attitude which, in turn, created a more positive and upbeat atmosphere. In January, with this in mind, I introduced what I designated as Project Snowball of Kindness and asked students what they thought it might mean. We talked about how a snowball continues to increase in size as it rolls through snowdrifts. Students then came to the conclusion that we could increase the circle of kindness by demonstrating a willingness to help others at school and at home.

It was determined that each child in our classroom would be responsible for selecting and scheduling their volunteer time of thirty minutes per week to help someone at school or at home. Students enthusiastically brainstormed who they would contact to arrange a time, convenient for both parties (being cautious not to interfere with academics). Students chose a variety of ways to volunteer such as assisting in the front office, reshelving books in the Media Center, helping the custodians, reading to Kindergarten classes, assisting a former teacher, one on one tutoring, and helping in a class for severely handicapped students.

Each child kept track of their visits and time spent in their Kindness Folder. Children loved sharing their experiences orally as well as in their writings. Parents were very supportive and were pleased to see their children involved in Project Snowball of Kindness which continued until the end of the school year.

I remember one particular child who was "all boy" through and through and who loved helping in a self contained classroom for students within the Severe and Profound range. He was very kind and patient and always looked forward to his weekly visits. The students in this class were thrilled and happy to see him each week. At the end of the school year, this volunteer child's mother came in to speak with the school principal to request that he be allowed to continue volunteering during the next school year because it had made such a difference in his life, as well as those he had helped.

Students felt proud of their efforts and experienced a great sense of accomplishment by participating in this project. It is my hope that these early seeds of kindness and volunteerism will continue to have an influence on these individuals as they grow into adulthood. From what I personally witnessed, the project turned out far beyond my expectations. Tuning in to my students' interests paid off.

Cissy Nichols, third grade teacher

Serious Day

As a high school physical educator, I hear all kinds of stories from my students about what they are going through or have been through. Every semester in my health classes I have what I call the "serious day" during a unit focused on relationships, specifically family relationships. I have heard all types of stories from students who were physically abused, students who were on serious drugs, students who have been scarred from verbal abuse, and even a few young ladies who have been willing to share with their classmates and teacher that they had been raped. Several students have been told by their parents or loved ones that they are no good, that they will never amount to anything. It is during these stories told firsthand by students that you begin to realize that life can be very difficult, and that so often we take our "good" lives for granted. Keep in mind, these are normally 14 or 15 year old kids.

On one particular "serious day," we had a very emotional day. Let me preface this by saying that I share a lot about my childhood before I open up the floor. Mostly I share some of the things I've been through so that they can see that I am human. One young lady had shared that she was physically abused by her father growing up. Another student shared about being addicted to methamphetamines (at one time) about six months before she shared with us. Yes, a 15 year old girl. Then, the already emotional class heard the story of all stories from a young lady I will call "Susie" for confidentiality reasons. As tears began to well up in everyone's eyes, including my own, Susie shared about how she had been molested from a very young age up until about three months prior to her sharing with the class. She shared the pain that she had been through and the guilt she felt inside because she felt that she was worthless. As she spoke between the tears and choked from crying vigorously, she made the story even more shocking. She had been molested by her female cousin. As the young lady choked up tears, students began to comfort her and offer her encouragement. I gathered myself and thanked the young lady for sharing. The counselors were made aware of the situation and she got the help that she needed.

A few weeks later, we went through our abstinence-based sex education curriculum called Choosing the Best. As our school nurse was going over the Sexually Transmitted Disease unit, Susie came to me and asked me to talk to the nurse about being tested. Susie and I went to the nurse and an STD test was arranged. Fortunately, the STD test came back negative for Susie. She was so happy to know that she was free from diseases. Up until the point where she heard about STD's in class, she had never thought about the fact that she could possibly have an STD.

From that day on, Susie has had some rough days for sure, but she has been seen far more often than not with a smile on her face. She always comes up and gives me hugs or simply shouts a "hey Coach Holmes" from down the hall. However, the best and most important thing to me is that Susie often thanks me for being a positive influence on her life. Many educators, administrators, etc. believe it is not our role to be a friend to our students. I disagree. I believe that we should be positive influences on these young people because we never know, unless they share with us, what they are going through. When young people see that we care about them, it results in their caring about you and respecting you. I will continue to teach this way regardless of what school or school system I'm teaching in. To put it simply, I do not have "serious days" for my own satisfaction. I want young people to see what their peers are going through, and that many times, some of the trivial things that they may be going through doesn't compare to the pain someone else has to go through or has been through. It just so happens that on this particular "serious day" this young lady helped me reinforce the main reason why I teach...having a positive impact on today's young people. The only way that can happen is to listen and respond.

Alex Holmes, high school physical educator

Knowledge Generator

As a high school social studies teacher, I have found two ways to almost guarantee successful connecting with students as they learn to connect with knowledge in using two techniques, "A Search for Knowledge" and "Facts in Five".

High school students are notoriously reticent to participate actively in classroom discussions, usually fearful of embarrassing themselves in front of their peers and friends. To remove one barrier that inhibits many students – the fear that they will give an incorrect response – I frequently employ an ad hoc cooperative learning activity that I call "A Search for Knowledge." I usually use it when I want students to compile some specific information, draw general conclusions, or simply to complete some activity. When directed to conduct a search for knowledge, all students simultaneously stand and begin to randomly move about the room, sharing and discussing information, and comparing and completing answers. Students are instructed to meet with as many other students as possible, frequently being coaxed to circulate and find another partner or group. I usually roam about the room, joining in some conversations if appropriate, but generally just assuring all students are on task. I only expend a short time on this activity, usually terminating it before students are able to fully coordinate a uniform response. Students respond well to this very informal activity, and the results are always quite satisfactory.

When I determine that the search is completed, students return to their seats, prepared to participate in a follow-up discussion. Flushed with confidence that they understand whatever task was assigned, or at least aware that no one else displayed a better response, normally uncommunicative students are anxious to respond aloud and participate in an open discussion. I especially like to employ a search for knowledge when I am being observed or evaluated because it appears to be quite chaotic and unorganized, but always proves itself to be effective.

When I was younger, I enjoyed a popular information game called "Facts in Five". The longer I teach, the more I realize that many classroom activities can be summarized in a concise list of five facts. I frequently ask students for "facts in five" at different junctures during instruction. The most obvious point for this technique is at the end of class to summarize five significant facts gleaned from the day's activities, but it can also be effective at the beginning of class to review previous instruction. I especially like this simple technique after a video or music selection or to wrap-up some other activity. It can also be used to set up new instruction, especially to uncover prior knowledge and to encourage discussion and participation. For example, "Facts in Five" can be initially introduced by teasing students with a requirement to name five of the Seven Dwarfs; their satisfaction with easily accomplishing the task can be quickly redirected by asking them to name five Supreme Court justices. This introduction can be adapted to any subject, but this trite example demonstrates how "Facts in Five" can generate a powerful mini-lecture, promote discussion, and intensify learning.

Both of these techniques are actually ways of seeking gifts of knowledge and sometimes discovering far more than expected as students demonstrate their new found knowledge.

Tip Hansen, high school history teacher

Morning Blunder

Each morning I write a morning message to my first graders that we read as a class. It tells them what we will be studying, informs them of any special events, and addresses any problems that need to be discussed. At the beginning of the year, I just read the message to them. Now they are at the point that they can read it to me. Anyway, on this particular Friday morning, I did not get a chance to write a morning message to my students. So as each one discovered my fault, they were eager to announce my mistake.

When we sat down for the morning meeting, I informed my students that for the first time all year I wasn't able to write a message that morning. One of my students blurted out, "We can write the message to you!" Everyone was in agreement and they enthusiastically set out to write a message to me. As the students took turns writing parts of the message, we were able to review various writing lessons such as: when to use a capital letter, correct punctuation, handwriting, etc. I didn't know that my students looked forward to reading the messages and it was rewarding to watch them get excited about working together to write a message back to me!

Since this serendipitous moment, I have decided to occasionally "forget" to write the message so that we can do more shared writings of the morning message.

Sarah Petersohn, first grade teacher

Protractors, Please

Several years ago I taught a third grade gifted math class. This was a great opportunity because it presented an occasion where we could cover material at a gifted pace and enrich whenever possible or appropriate. On one particular day we were discussing angles and identifying whether or not they were less than 90 degrees or greater than 90 degrees. This was all that the third grade skills and objectives mandated that we do. In fact, in the text the angles were not even called by their geometric names (acute and obtuse).

Anyway, we continued with our discussion and exercises in our book with additional examples on the board. As we were nearing the end of our class period, a student raised his hand and asked a very interesting question. He said, "Ms. Straner, how do you know exactly what size the angles are?" WOW! I love questions like this one. My only problem that day was that our class time was over, and we didn't have time to pursue the question. I promised the child that the next day we would be learning to determine the size of angles. A big grin crossed his face as he left the classroom anticipating tomorrow's adventure.

I could not let this opportunity go by. In preparing for the class the next day, I located my trusty protractors, created an activity sheet of angles for my students to measure, and readied myself for a new adventure. My students came to math the next day already excited because we were going to do something new and different. What fun we did have!

I demonstrated for my students the way to measure angles. We talked about how to draw angles as well, and we talked about the correct names for each. We had such a great class that day. Once they measured the angles I had created for them, they wanted to draw their own. My response was "Help yourself!" Now we could talk about angles in an intelligent way. So, we practiced, "An acute angle is less than 90 degrees. An obtuse angle is greater than 90 degrees, but less than 180 degrees. A right angle is exactly 90 degrees, and a straight angle is 180 degrees."

My students gained new knowledge that day and found something exciting they could share and talk about. I have often thought about what would have happened if I had simply said, "Oh, you will learn that in a year or two." I can tell you what would have happened. We would have missed a great spontaneous learning opportunity which not only enhanced their math skills, but also enriched their vocabulary. I decided that it was okay that my lesson plans didn't say that we would measure angles. We were learning.....and we were excited about what we were doing. Now, that's serendipity!

Joy Straner, teacher of third grade gifted class

Our shared stories from different grades, subjects, and demographics serve to show you that anyone can find serendipity if you are seeking it. These positive experiences are to remind (and inspire) us that our greatest purpose is for the benefit of the students.

The Connection Factor: Seeking Serendipity

Chapter Eight
Making a Difference

Making a difference...isn't that what it's all about? We didn't exactly decide to teach students as a get-rich scheme! So, how can we make a difference in students' learning and in their lives? We hope we've given you a lot to think about already in regards to our Serendipity Principle and suggested teaching strategies. You can teach *at* students all day every day, exposing them to all the required performance standards, but may never make a dent in their absorbing the information and then retaining it, if you don't connect with students and apply certain traits as you teach.

Remember that teacher in your past who was extraordinary? Let's consider traits of that teacher and other extraordinary teachers. For those of you who did not recall an outstanding teacher, it may have been because your teachers did not demonstrate traits that assured students the awareness that their teachers cared about them. Students are not going to care if you don't let them know you do!

Compassion (or caring about your students as real people) is a part of that connection factor to which we have referred. If you don't tune in to students as people, noting their interests, aptitudes and needs, you stand a good chance of losing them. Tune in to them - so they will tune in to you and to learning. How do extraordinary teachers do that? We are listing some of our own ideas that we believe answer this question.

• They look at students in the eyes with pleasant expressions which make them a warmer and more approachable teacher.

• They listen to students' responses and really pay attention to what they say.

• They show concern when a student is "missing the boat" and try to help them "get it".

• They smile frequently to help provide a happy warm environment.

• They use humor appropriately to help students have fun.

• They encourage students, rather than intimidate.

• They are patient and kind even when it takes everything they've got to be so.

• They use effective classroom management in order to minimize discipline problems.

• They plan in ways that will reach all students.

• They help students make sense of why they are learning so that they can apply the learning to their present and future lives.

• They demonstrate personal high values, and in doing so, serve as effective role models for their students.

• They relax with the students as much as possible rather

than the alternative of displaying too much intensity about what they're trying to accomplish with the students which can put undue pressure on students. When teachers feel the strain from expectations of the administration and the school system, it is natural (yet avoidable) to have this pressure flow downstream to the students. Do you function well with too much stress? No, and neither do our students.

Yes, we believe that many of these traits are in relation to the personality of the teacher and that using them always (or even often) is extremely difficult for some or many teachers. After all, just as students, teachers are fallible people who come in all shapes, sizes, and qualities. However, if a teacher makes a conscientious effort to apply these traits in their relationships with their students, it is possible to develop the habit of conducting themselves in these ways and – guess what? – it feels a lot better to apply these behaviors than the opposite behaviors. When you're encouraging, patient and caring (and all those above listed traits) towards students, they are more apt to want to attend your class and perform well. And, when anyone - any age - is learning in a relaxed, natural atmosphere, they are more likely to retain what they learn…hopefully, not only for testing purposes, but also for lifetime knowledge!

How do we authors know what works? Because after a combined sixty years of teaching, we, like many veteran teachers, have tried it all and have figured out what works best. And yes, we'll readily admit that it's not easy, but once you get into the right frame of mind as you display these characteristics of an extraordinary teacher, you will also know and want to apply what works! We have certainly made mistakes in our careers in handling situations and relationships with students. (Let us know someone who hasn't!) Trial and error can be our best tool for learning how to get things right, but it's not the only way to learn. Listen and learn from the experienced teachers who are willing to share as we are doing now! We emphasize that if you diligently try to be the teacher you know you can be, it is certainly possible to succeed at doing it.

It is our strong desire that more teachers in our great country remember what teaching is all about – the students.

We do not oppose performance standards because it is beneficial to have expectations in place so we know where we're aiming to go. You wouldn't set out for a journey without knowing the destination. However, our concern lies when there is too much emphasis on standards, test scores, and school failure/passing. Our nation has quickly and sadly moved away from the students as being individual people. These students all have feelings and individual goals just as students always have. And they are not all the same. Their backgrounds are vast – more diverse than ever. Some come from families who have reasonable goals for them. Some families put too much pressure on their children, and some do not even care how they perform or learn.

It is good to expect all students to read and possess other basic skills by graduation, but they are simply not all going to master every standard set before them; it is entirely unreasonable to expect that. If teachers put the demands on themselves to accomplish unreasonable, unattainable goals with their students, they will be miserable people who may give up and not carry out a lifetime career of teaching. Why? Because they will feel as though they are failures. If, however, teachers will reasonably approach goals, knowing they will do the best they can do to help each child reach them, they should feel good about whatever the outcomes are. "Don't sweat the small stuff!" Life will go on successfully for you as teachers if some students do not progress as well as you might hope. Even the students may be successful in life if they do not test well! Come on. Let's accept the fact that many successful people in this world did not knock the socks off at standardized test time! It's time to get real about this testing matter.

Let's focus on that word "relax" (as opposed to being too intense or frustrated). That's quite challenging if you're not a master at multi-tasking. One can become quite frustrated if that is the case! Yet it is a necessary skill in today's world of teaching. It can be learned if you find what's comfortable for you. Having mentors give you tips on juggling many tasks is a great way to improve, but be careful about comparing yourself to "master multi-taskers"! Doing so may frustrate you further. We are absolutely not all exceptional at that, so if this skill is too complex for you, limit your tasks in small chunks of time in order to help you lighten up! In other words, take it in baby steps instead of trying to climb an entire mountain in a short time.

And, take it easy. Think about how you'd like your students to remember you down the road. Do you want them to think of you as an uptight tyrant? We doubt it. Instead, you most likely prefer that they remember you as a caring, fun teacher who knew how to guide students towards success. Think about it. Are we right?

Okay, let's recap the process of guiding students towards success in ways we have suggested in this book.

- Keep the **Five Jewels** for effective classroom instruction in mind as a foundation for your teaching.

- Based on selected standards, plan effective lessons beginning with a **launcher** that will draw them into learning.

- While planning and teaching, remember to include **differentiation strategies** in order to reach all your students.

- Not only do learning styles and ability levels need to be considered, but also include **plans and strategies for language learners.**

- Keep **assessment** ongoing to drive your instruction based on the performance of your students.

- **Wrapping up** the major points at the end of your lesson is important to help students see the big picture and retain information. This is what we are doing right now for you!

- Focus on **"The Connection Factor"** and take advantage of those **"Serendipitous Moments"**.

If you give your students room to explore and learn on their own (with meaningful guidance from you), you will see serendipity stories almost daily. Your students will be learning in a happy, relaxed atmosphere because you have demonstrated extraordinary traits as you teach. You will have given them opportunities to grow as people as they buy in to their learning. This successful accomplishment of allowing these teachable moments to unexpectedly take off will give you purpose. This sense of purpose should eliminate burn-out and allow you to have a contented teaching career. We sincerely wish this for you and our nation's students.

In our view, job satisfaction in any career comes from helping others. Teaching is certainly no exception as it presents many opportunities for reaching out to children every day. Students of all ages need nurturing – some more than others. Teachers who effectively respond to these needs stand a better chance of receiving fulfillment in their own lives. We would like to share two stories to demonstrate how two educators responded to individual students who needed a compassionate mentor. Their acts of kindness and compassion made a life-changing difference in these students' futures. As we close with these stories, we challenge you to think about what might have happened in these students' lives if no positive intervention had taken place. Remember that there are times that a student's teacher may be the only person who is in a position to demonstrate a caring spirit and in doing so – make a difference in a student's life.

This story is in the form of a letter which was written by a former third grader to her former third grade teacher after her teacher recently lost her son to cancer. The letter was written fifty-three years after their third grade student-teacher relationship. The third grade student had suffered a traumatic family tragedy during that third grade year. The teacher's son, Brad, had been in the student's (Lynn's) graduating class.

Dear Rue,

You don't know how hard it is not to say 'Dear Mrs. Bradberry'. Your current name, Walker, is so unfamiliar to me, so I just said 'Rue'. I hope that is OK. My heart hurts for you. I remember a little third grade girl with a hurting heart that you reached out to many years ago. You helped put my pieces back together. Although you were unaware, part of your ministering to me was letting me rub your shoulders as you read the Bobbsey Twins to us everyday after lunch. You had no idea how much I needed that feeling of touch and bond because of my severe pain I had to endure that year. I always believed if I did an especially good job that you would read two chapters to us instead of only one. Sometimes it worked.

Right after the death of your son, I was in an antique shop and ran across this Bobbsey Twins book. It just seemed right for me to send it to you in thanks for taking such good care of me so long ago.

Maybe in a little way it will help your hurt by reminding you of how you helped me heal.

Brad was very special and much of that credit goes to you. His personality was so much a part of our high school class of 1963. We will miss him.

Love,
Lynn Baell Wilson

This letter demonstrates to us the importance of reaching out to hurting students whose pain can greatly affect their education and life. They are people too, and their family life (through no choice of their own) influences who they are in their school setting. It doesn't matter how well a teacher teaches if a teacher disregards their hurting spirits. The hurting student will most likely not respond until they have passed a certain point in their grieving period. This teacher, the former Mrs. Bradberry, obviously had great influence on this former student's life for her actions to have been so well remembered 53 years later. She innately knew the significance of tuning in to children's needs. This student, Lynn, benefited from her teacher's nurturing ways as she went on to learn and thrive.

Our final story shows a special connection between a coach and an athlete:

Mr. Jones, a principal, shared with his faculty at a staff meeting about Thomas, a former high school wrestling student. He mentioned that this student was not a good test taker and was at risk not to graduate. After many struggles with his studies and working hard with the wrestling team, Thomas triumphantly won the state championship. When Mr. Jones handed him a phone to call home to share the good news, he said to Thomas, "Tell the people you love what you have done!"

Thomas handed him back the phone and said, "You're standing here with me."

The Connection Factor:
Making a Difference

References

Adams, Cheryll M. and Rebecca L. Pierce. (2003). *Teaching by tiering*. NSTA News Digest, October 24, 2003.

Blum, Raymond. (1995). *Math tricks, puzzles, & games*. New York: Sterling Publishing Co., Inc.

Bolin, Frances Schoonmaker. (1995). *Poetry for young people: Carl Sandburg*. New York: Scholastic, Inc.

Brumbaugh, Doug and Linda, and Rock, David. (2001). *Scratch your brain*. Pacific Grove, California: Critical Thinking Books and Software.

Burnette, Jane. (1999). *Critical behaviors and strategies for teaching culturally diverse students*. ERIC Digest #ED435147, November 1999.

Cox, Carole. (2008). *Teaching language arts: a student-centered classroom*. Boston: Pearson Education, Inc.

Cummins, J. (1992). *The multicultural classroom: readings for content-area teachers* (pp. 16-26). White Plains, NY: Longman.

Godwin, Johnnie C. (2000). *Life's best chapter: retirement*. Birmingham, Alabama. New Hope Publishers.

Hardin, Carlette Jackson. (2008). *Effective classroom management*. Upper Saddle River, New Jersey: Pearson Education, Inc.

Hoffman, J., Assaf, L., Pennington, J., & Paris, S. G. (2001). *High stakes testing in reading: today in texas, tomorrow. Reading Teacher,* 54, 482-492.

Jameson, Judy. (2004). www.ets.org (The Florida and the Islands Comprehensive Center at ETS).

Johnson, D., Johnson, R., & Holobec, E. (1991). *Cooperation in the classroom*. Edina, MN: Interaction Book.

Kottler, Ellen and Gallavan, Nancy P. (2007). *Secrets to success for beginning elementary school teachers*. Thousand Oaks, California. Corwin Press: Sage Publications Company.

Manheim, Ralph and Mok, Michel. (1994). *Anne Frank's tales from the secret annex*. New York: Bantam Books.

Marzano, R. J. (2000). *Transforming classroom grading*. Alexandria, VA: Association for Supervision and Curriculum Development.

Novak, J.D. and Gowin, D.B. (1984). *Learning how to learn.* Cambridge and NY: Cambridge University Press.

Pease, Gene. (2008). Education professor, Piedmont College, Demorest, Georgia.

Popham, W. James. (2003). *If I Were America's Assessment Czar.* Large-Scale Assessment Conference. San Antonio, TX. June 23 -26, 2003.

Powell, Sara Davis. (2009). *An introduction to education: choosing your teaching path.* Upper Saddle River, New Jersey: Pearson Education, Inc.

Sloane, Paul and MacHale, Des. (1993). *Challenging lateral thinking puzzles.* New York: Sterling Publishing Co., Inc.

Straner, T. Joy and White, Dawn (2001). *Pele's Peak: a thematic unit that brings volcanoes alive for your students.* Carlsbad, California: Interaction Publishers, Inc.

Theroux, Priscilla. (2004). www.members.shaw.ca/priscillatheroux/brain.html. Alberta, Canada.

Tierney, R. J., Johnston, P., Moore, D. W., & Valencia, S. W. (2000). *Snippets: how will literacy be assessed in the next millennium?* Reading Research Quarterly, 35, 244-250.

Tomlinson, Carol Ann. (1995). *Differentiating instruction for advanced learners in the mixed-ability middle school classroom.* ERIC EC Digest #E536, October 1995.

Tomlinson, Carol Ann. (1999). *The differentiated classroom: responding to the needs of all learners.* Alexandria, VA: Association for Supervision and Curriculum Development.

Tomlinson, Carol Ann. (2000). *Differentiation of instruction in the elementary grades.* ERIC Digest. ERIC Clearinghouse on Elementary and Early Childhood Education.

Wiggins, G. P. and J. McTighe. (2004). *Understanding by design.* Alexandria, VA: ASCD.

Willis, Scott and Larry Mann. (2000). *Differentiating instruction.* Curriculum Update, Winter 2000.

Wong, Harry K. and Rosemary T. (2001). *How to be an effective teacher: the first days of school.* Mountain View, California: Harry K. Wong Publications, Inc.

www.ets.org (The Florida and the Islands Comprehensive Center at ETS)
www.readingrockets.org
www.usconstitution.net/constmiss.html

Appendix A

Benjamin Bloom's Hierarchy of Thinking

Evaluation – Development of Opinions, Judgments or Decisions
Do you agree or disagree and why?
What do you think about _____?
What is the most important _____ and why?
What criteria would you use to assess _____?

Synthesis – Combination of Ideas to Form a New Whole
What would you predict/infer from _____?
How would you create/design a new _____?
What might happen if you combined _____ with _____?
What if I eliminated a part?
What if I reversed or rearranged?
What solutions would you suggest for _____?

Analysis – Separation of a Whole into Component Parts
Classify _____ according to _____.
Outline/Diagram/Web
How does _____ compare/contrast with _____?
What evidence can you present for _____?

Application – Use of Facts, Rules, Principles
How is _____ an example of _____?
How is _____ related to _____?

Comprehension – Organization and Selection of Facts and Ideas
Retell (in your own words)
What is the main idea of _____?

Knowledge – Identification and Recall of Information
Who, What, When, Where, How, Describe, List

Appendix B

Additional Resources for Differentiation

Use the following web sites for additional information on differentiating the curriculum in your classrooms.

www.ascd.org
> This site has books, videos, etc. related to differentiation.

Education Insights
> This site has interviews in the educational field.

Differentiation Toolbox
> This is a great site with links to information and articles as well as templates for planning tiered lessons and other charts for planning purposes.

www.bsu.edu/teachers/services/ctr/javits
> This gives you suggested resources for anchoring activities.

And don't forget the following can give you additional activities for varied use in your classrooms. Podcasts are great in the field of social studies with current news events from CNN. Other available resources include: PBS television, Web Casts, United Streaming and Brain Pop.

Appendix C

Examples of Differentiating Content, Process, Product, and Learning Environment

By: Carol Ann Tomlinson (2000)

Content:

1. Using reading materials at varying readability levels.

2. Putting text materials on tape.

3. Using spelling or vocabulary lists at readiness levels of students.

4. Presenting ideas through both auditory and visual means.

5. Using reading buddies.

6. Meeting with small groups to re-teach an idea or skill for struggling learners, or to extend the thinking or skills of advanced learners.

Process:

1. Using tiered activities through which all learners work with the same important understandings and skills, but proceed with different levels of support, challenge, or complexity.

2. Providing interest centers that encourage students to explore subsets of the class topic of particular interest to them.

3. Developing personal agendas (task lists written by the teacher and containing both in-common work for the whole class and work that addresses individual needs to learners) to be completed either during specified agenda time or as students complete other work early.

4. Offering manipulatives or other hands-on supports for students who need them.

5. Varying the length of time a student may take to complete

a task in order to provide additional support for a struggling learner or to encourage an advanced learner to pursue a topic in greater depth.

Products:

1. Giving students options of how to express required learning (e.g., create a puppet show, write a letter, or develop a mural with labels).

2. Using rubrics that match and extend students' varied skills levels.

3. Allowing students to work alone or in small groups on their products.

4. Encouraging students to create their own product assignments as long as the assignments contain required elements.

Learning Environment:

1. Making sure there are places in the room to work quietly and without distraction, as well as places that invite student collaboration;

2. Providing materials that reflect a variety of cultures and home settings;

3. Setting out clear guidelines for independent work that matches individual needs;

4. Developing routines that allow students to get help when teachers are busy with other students and cannot help them immediately; and

5. Helping students understand that some learners need to move around to learn, while others do better sitting quietly.

Excerpted from: Tomlinson, C.A. (August, 2000). Differentiation of Instruction in the Elementary Grades. ERIC Digest. ERIC Clearinghouse on Elementary and Early Childhood Education. http://www.readingrockets.org

124

Appendix D

Group Presentation Rubric
U.S. Constitution Mini-Unit

Student Name: _____ Date: _____

Criteria Evaluated	Not Satisfactory 1	Minimally Adequate 2	Meets Expectations 3	Exceeds Expectations 4	Total
Clarity of Presentation Topic	Topic not clear; research not sufficient	Topic focused and researched acceptably	Topic consistently focused and researched well	Topic well developed and researched commendably	
Supporting Details Organized Evidence of details connecting to topic should be present.	Details completed in a confusing manner; not well planned	Most details presented well; satisfactory presentation, but nothing to make it stand out	Details clearly communicated; effective planning evident; catches audience's attention; content expressed well	Details communicated superbly; exceptional content; stands out from the rest	
Oral Presentation with Creative Component Creative component must be either drama, music, or other approved component.	Creative component was absent or poor; not creatively planned	Satisfactory use of creative component	Creative component well planned; good idea to use with your topic	Exceptional creative presentation	
Presentation Visual This needs to be a poster or art piece or a graphic organizer that helps classmates understand your topic.	Visual was absent or poor; does not enhance topic	Visual satisfactorily adds to topic	Effective use of visual with topic; visual well done	Extraordinary use of visual aid to enhance topic!	

Total Score: _____

About the Authors

Joy Straner instructs and supervises part time at Piedmont College (Georgia) in the Department of Education after recently completing 30 years of public school teaching in Georgia. She taught in K-12 and ended her public school career teaching elementary school which included both regular and gifted education. Among her accomplishments she was selected Stephens County Teacher of the Year in 1992, she received the state curriculum award in 1999 from the Georgia Association for Gifted Children for co-writing an interactive brain-based curriculum, she won the 2000 Gifted Program Teacher of the Year award from the Gwinnett Association for Gifted Education and was accepted as part of the Teachers as Leaders Class of 2000. She co-authored an interactive curriculum unit entitled *Pele's Peak* which was published by Interact in 2001. Ms. Straner holds a Bachelor of Arts degree in English and Journalism from Tift College of Mercer University, a Masters degree in Elementary Education from Clemson University, and an Educational Specialists degree in Administration and Supervision from Lincoln Memorial University.

Beth Bloodworth Threlkeld has supervised and instructed at Piedmont College as a part time education instructor for three years after 30 years of teaching in the public schools in Georgia. She taught in the regular classrooms of both elementary and middle grades. Fourteen years were spent as a certified teacher of English Language Learners (ELL). As Lawrenceville Middle School's PTA President, she co-founded and then co-sponsored for ten years Stride which was a county/state/national award-winning student-teacher effort to promote drug-free lives. In 1996 Beth served as a Georgia TESOL (Teachers of English Speakers of Other Languages) Elementary Interest Section Co-leader. In 2003-04 she was chosen as J.G. Dyer Elementary School's Teacher of the Year and was a semi-finalist for the Gwinnett County Teacher of the Year. Beth received her Bachelor of Science degree in Elementary Education and her Masters in Education from the University of Georgia. She holds an Educational Specialist degree in Administration and Supervision from Lincoln Memorial University.

The authors have worked jointly on research projects both in the university setting in Tennessee and the Gwinnett School System in Georgia. Their experiences have been both varied and similar. Joy and Beth each have 30 years of teaching experience in elementary, middle and/or high schools. Beth's expertise falls in the area of English Language Learners with Joy's expertise coming in the area of gifted education. They have both been privileged to speak or present at local, state, and/or national conventions/conferences. Their educational zeal now is working with teacher candidates at the college level. This opportunity enables them to continue to be a part of the education arena where their desire is to share experiences and expertise in the field of teaching. Working in the college setting has confirmed to the authors that students' individual needs can better be met when teachers connect with their students. This book is a culmination of their work and their passion...a dream fulfilled as they have created this idea of The Connection Factor and Serendipity Teaching.

LaVergne, TN USA
06 July 2010

188438LV00004B/45/P